MW01204485

THE PROFESSOR AND THE ENGLISH SPY

Memoir of a World War II French/Italian Underground Journey ~ 1942-1944

by

Samuel Berlin

.

Copyright © 2012 by Samuel Berlin

All rights reserved.

ISBN: 1477647112

ISBN-13: 9781477647110

For my loving mother who,

through my childhood,

taught me tolerance.

ACKNOWLEDGMENTS

I extend my sincere gratitude to family and friends who finally persuaded me to write this memoir; namely: My children, Renée M. Sera, Amy A. Berlin, Jeffrey A. Berlin, and Dr. Ross D. Berlin for their support, assistance and continued encouragement; my wife, Helen Berlin, for her undying dedication and indefatigable persistence in seeing this project come to full fruition; my friend and golfing partner, John Hochuli, who, over the *course* of years, has listened to my war stories and insisted that I set them down on paper; my editor, Robert J. Banfelder, who, along with Helen, made the process painless—while I played golf.

Finally, I humbly acknowledge all those folks (too numerous to list), peasants and partisans alike, who put their lives at risk to assist Pierre and me. I wouldn't be here if not for them. You will meet these fearless people upon the pages that follow.

Samuel Berlin

CHAPTER ONE

My concerns and anxiety were building by the minute.

"Ma, the fellows of the underground told me that they're going to have a raid, for sure. Please, let's do something about it." My mother looked at me with eyes that parents give their kids when they want to say, *You're so young; what do you know? I'm so much older than you are, my boy, so I'll tolerate your remark.* "Ma, the men reported that it's going to be a big raid because Joseph, whose father is on the police force, said that the German *Kommandant* said that the entire police force has to be available tonight to assist in the raid. Ma, please!"

Again, the same *What-do-you-know?* look. "You're only seventeen years old, and you make it sound as if the Russian pogroms are going to take place again."

She pulled my head down upon her shoulder while I held my mother around her ample waist. For a fleeting moment, I felt safe—like when I was little and she would put my face into her big, warm comforting bosom. I would find all sorts of excuses to remain in that lovely, blissful position for as long as possible.

"Ma." I spoke very quietly now. "This is really serious. I feel it, Ma. Let's go away to the country; let's do something."

"What is destined for us will happen no matter what we do. It's entirely in the hands of the Almighty because He makes all the plans."

I knew then that anything else I would say would be wasted energy. So we held each other a little longer while she gently rocked me. Oh, how I loved her even when she hit me because I did something to upset her. I had to laugh because she complained bitterly each time that she hit one of my bones, and I would grab her by the wrists and pin them behind her back. Oh, how she protested vehemently and called me a no-goodnik, a bum. At the same time, she would start laughing and tell me to stop it, to go away and leave her alone. But there was no physical protest on her part. When I released her, invariably she would grab my head and give me a kiss in the most unlikely place. I remember once when I thought she was going for my ear but somehow, midway, she must have changed her mind because she went straight for my eye. I was totally unprepared. I couldn't see for days, and my eye was continuously tearing. Reared from Russian peasant stock, her love was rough-and-tumble as was her vocabulary.

When I walked away from such an encounter, I grew at least ten feet tall. My mother's demeanor was, for the most part, stoical. Yet, she was capable of shedding a tear, especially when she talked about her sisters and her father. Her father was dead a long time, and we had a big picture of him on the wall. My mother always said to me that I looked exactly like him, and I liked that. I don't know why, but it always pleased me when Ma looked at me with wet moist eyes and, after awhile, said, "Yes, you look just like your grandfather." There was nothing else to be said.

My father and I, unfortunately, didn't get along. He seemed to be omnipresent and unquestionably overbearing, hitting me with his hands, a stick, or whatever lay nearby—certain to be broken across my back or atop my head. He was not only a most angry man but also stupid and cowardly. This is a true statement and not one that comes from any hate or revenge. When I was very young, I came home with a complaint about one of my teachers, and my father concluded that if my teacher punished me, I was deserving of it. He promptly proceeded to whip me on my buttocks with his belt, closing the door to any potential father and son relationship. After a few other incidents, that door was closed forever.

Too, our family relationship grew dark and felt very uncomfortable. One day my mother went to fill the kettle for tea. My father had just walked in from the backyard. When the water was hot, Ma filled her cup. "You want some tea, Sam?" she asked me.

"No thank you, Ma."

She did not offer my father anything. They were not on good speaking terms and were constantly fighting.

"Why don't you ask *me* if *I* want tea?" my father asked sullenly.

"You can get your own," Ma said flatly.

"Fine. I don't think you appreciate what I do for this family. Do you think it is easy making a living from a pushcart in the open market while standing in the hot sun and the cold weather all day, six days a week? And these women. If I show them a white tablecloth with blue flowers, they ask me if I have a yellow one with red flowers. The curtains I show them are too long, too , too thick or too thin, and then I come home to a big-mouth wife. Pah! God save me from such a life!"

"And I spend my days sewing shirts for people who also complain," Ma retorted. "'The collar on this shirt is too small,' 'too big,' they say. The sleeves are either too long or too . I feel sorry for both of us. And we take people in for a few days' rest; then they move on to somewhere else. Where? I can't feed them. I can't even feed myself. My son tells me he is not hungry when I offer him a second slice of bread because he knows there may not be anymore bread until next week. The women come with big bellies. Where will they have their babies? In the street with the rats? What is happening?"

She sat at the table, quietly sipping her tea. My father was reading the paper, and I just looked at them, thinking to myself about the wasted energy they spent, silently or openly fighting with each other, constantly, sometimes over the most trivial things. My father, like Ma, also came from Russian peasant stock; however, he wanted to hide that fact, but I could not understand why that was so. My mind returned to the moment at hand.

"Pa, as I told Ma, there is going to be a raid tonight. We should leave right now and come back when it's over,"

I repeated.

My father smirked. "Do you think this is Russia with the Cossacks? What are you afraid of? It won't happen here. This is a civilized land. There are laws," he chastised.

"There is a German army in the land!" I exclaimed.

"You don't know anything. Nothing is going to happen. Nothing," Pa declared. "Belgium is not Russia. How stupid can you get?"

I heard the grandfather clock chiming. I never counted the strokes; however, each time I heard the slow ding-dong resounding through the room, I felt good inside. There were times I didn't hear the hourly chime. I would ask if the clock was broken. I was relieved to learn that the clock just needed to be wound.

That evening, the last chime faded away . . . when suddenly it happened. We all looked at one another and didn't move. Someone was banging hard on the door. I sensed the worst.

"*Aufmachen!*"

Someone was now banging violently upon the door. My father and mother jumped up, and for the first time in my life I saw my father take her into his arms.

"It's the pogroms again, Rose," Pa said.

"Oh, my all merciful God, protect us," Ma whispered.

My father looked at me and said, "Open the door before they break it down."

I quickly got up and ran through the long corridor. The door started to give in at one of its hinges. "All right, I'm opening up." I had to pull the door hard because it was stuck on the bottom. When I finally managed to pull it open wide, I saw them standing there: two men wearing long brown leather coats, pistols drawn. Behind the pair, stood Joseph's father.

One of the soldiers shone a flashlight in my face. *The bloody bastards.*

"Where is everybody?" they demanded, pushing me aside, walking in and down along the corridor.

My parents came out of the kitchen, still holding each other. What a sight. They were literally supporting one another. It was a symbiotic moment that couldn't be replicated. Still staring, I had momentarily forgotten the German roaches in their long coats. Then one of the leeches spoke to Joseph's father in German, instructing him to tell my parents to get ready in five minutes, to come with them with extra clothing. Joseph's father, the policeman, with an expression of complete helplessness, translated in Flemish, and very quietly added, "I'm so sorry, but I have to assist them. I have no choice."

Then one of the varmints turned to me and asked if I was going with my parents, and out of a corner of my eye, I saw my father motion to me in the negative.

I was born in Belgium, and a citizen. At that particular point in time, 1942, the Germans did not deport Jews of Belgian nationality. I responded through Joseph's father that I wasn't going with them, and in German one of the soldiers replied, "Then we'll get you later." The bastard didn't know that I spoke German. We had Jewish refugees from Germany staying in our home from time to time, and because of my knowledge of Yiddish, it was a cinch to learn German. Also, I spoke several languages reasonably well.

I saw my parents starting to put some clothing in a bed sheet, when all of a sudden the soldiers motioned with their pistols for them to come immediately.

"Come on, let's go, that's it, five minutes are over." It wasn't even one minute.

My father came over to me, embraced me and whispered in my ear, "Under the mattress, five thousand francs."

Then my mother embraced me, and as we held each other for just a moment, the cockroach tore us apart.

Suddenly, I was an orphan. Alone, all alone, I stood there in a complete state of shock. I told myself I'd soon awake and tell my mother about this terrible nightmare— the banging and breaking in of the front door. And she would calm me and tell me that my dream was manifested by a big storm with heavy rains, thunder and lightening. *That was the banging and other noises you heard in your dream*, she would hopefully explain. But I was awake. Reality had set in, and the Nazis did take my parents away. Never again would I nestle my face against my mother's bosom. Never again would my father hit me. The front door *was* hanging on one hinge . . . and I was, forever, an orphan. Alone. All alone.

I walked upstairs to my room and heard screaming from the street: "Please don't take me!" Cries. Moaning. "Don't hit my father! Please stop!" Eventually, the cries and moans became unintelligible; raw animal sounds coming from screaming humans. *Why, for God's sake, why?* I asked myself. The answer came quickly. *Because they had the guns pointed at us*, I realized. It was just that simple: the guns, knives, boots—the Nazis. *Curses on your rotten, twisted minds. Curses on the sound from your boots. From the dregs of the earth you come, put on a uniform then point a pistol. Garbage . . . debris of humanity. Curses on all of you.* My heart was full of hate.

They took my mother away and they must pay. I fell down on my bed and cried because I was alone and felt so abandoned. I was an orphan. Upon awakening the next day, I again wondered if it had all been a dream. It must have been, but that illusion lasted for no more than a blink of an eye. Suddenly, it hit me. What was I to do? I never had to deal with anything like this before. Maybe if I went outside, I could find someone to talk to: a neighbor or a friend. Someone.

I dressed and went downstairs to my parents' bedroom, which faced the street. I looked outside and saw blood on the five steps leading to the house of my friend, a deaf mute. His father made a modest living sewing buttonholes. It was on those very steps that I would gather with other neighborhood kids, to tell off-color jokes and to look at racy French pictures. How we laughed on those steps. How I enjoyed the Belgian sun when it was about to dip beneath the houses. My own steps were stained by blood, and it was on the sidewalk as well as the walls. I wanted to steal a tank and drive it up to the German *Kommandant,* right up to the front of their building and shoot with unerring marksmanship, making them bleed until they looked like chickens in a slaughterhouse hanging upside down, lifeless, so that they could never hurt anyone ever again. Oh, I felt so helpless.

I must go to the city park, which was situated about a fifteen-minute walk from where I lived, practically in the heart of Antwerp. The front door was askew, half lying half standing. Poor door, which normally I could close with one finger until the lock caught. Poor broken door. Even you they didn't spare. The Nazis are the worst because when they start breaking down doors, nothing is sacred. It is the end of civilization.

I walked quickly through the empty streets, made a few turns and arrived at the park. I had the presence of mind to take off the yellow Star of David. I knew that if I would be seen with that symbol, it would mean the end for me, too. My blood would be added to that of my friends and neighbors.

CHAPTER TWO

Having arrived at the entrance to the park, there was a sign that was all too familiar, and it hurt me deeply. The sign read: Dogs and Jews are forbidden to enter the park. *To hell with them*, I thought. *This is my park, and I'm going in.* I walked along empty paths, sat down, watched the birds, and my heart started to hurt again. I just let my emotions go, walked up to the old chestnut tree and wrapped my arms around its welcoming trunk and cried again. All of a sudden I heard laughter. I quickly disengaged myself from the trunk, wiped my eyes, blew my nose and looked in the direction of the laughter.

"Hey, Günther," I called out. "What are you doing here?" What a stupid question. But that was the only thing I thought to ask my friend, with whom I sometime worked in the trade school and occasionally played soccer. Today, he appeared different. He was flanked by two laughing girls. The three were wearing black and brown uniforms. Günther had on boots, and a knife was hanging from his side. A leather strap crossed his chest. *What happened to his hair?* I wondered. All those nice beautiful blond waves were gone. It was so strange. Suddenly, he spoke to me.

"You fucking Jew. Don't you know you can't come in here? Get out before I cut you down."

The girls laughed. Günther stood with his legs spread and his thumbs hooked onto his belt. I had heard this insult said to me many times, but never in such an open, inflammatory fashion.

When I went to trade school, there were about fifteen Jewish students among fifteen hundred, and I had to fight my way through school. There was always a fresh challenge. Someone who thought he could beat me. But I was six feet tall and an accomplished gymnast and swimmer. I wasn't afraid of a fight and usually emerged the victor. That was even before I heard the words karate or judo. I instinctively knew the power of the elbow, the edge of my palm, and the side or the heel of my foot. I was always effective, and I never used any more force than was absolutely necessary. I remember one fight I had with a guy who physically abused a friend of mine. My friend was so gentle, and whatever he lacked in physical prowess, he made up for in mental acuity. It was a mean fight that I had with my friend's abuser, lasting but fifteen seconds. The next time I met him at the top of the stairs in school, he had his arm in a sling, and his face looked as if he had been caught in a mangle. I remember having gone over to him with my hand extended, asking for his friendship. He called me some name, which made my blood boil, and I promptly threw him down the stairs.

My poor mother would always go out of her mind whenever I came home from a fight with a swollen cheek or a shiner.

"What do you mean you didn't see where you were going?" she would question. "What door slammed your nose?"

After several incidents, she knew what had happened. However, it was against her upbringing to endorse any kind of physical expression. She'd argue, "Let them call you what they want. Just mind your own business and keep on going."

But this encounter with Günther in the park was different because he had a knife and was wearing a uniform and boots. I was a stranger in the country where I was born. My eyes were wet from anger. My hands itched to smash his grinning face. I recall the tension in my clenched fists. Following my mother's advice, I let him call me what he wanted. I minded my own business, turned around and kept on going until I was outside of what used to be *my* park. I now knew for sure what I had to do—keep on going—but this time it had to be for a long distance because I wouldn't be able to stay here any longer.

Upon arriving home, I looked under my parents' mattress and found a brown bag filled with Belgian paper money, about five thousand francs—the money my father had spoken of before the Germans took him and Ma away. I took a burlap bag that once contained onions, filling it with cans of beans, ersatz bread and other food articles. I put on my cap and, without lingering another unnecessary moment, walked out of my home of seventeen years.

I reached the corner of my street and turned around for a final time, staring back at the hanging door to my home before rapidly walking to the main train station in Antwerp. South was my destination to Nice, the part of France where the Italian occupation had jurisdiction.

CHAPTER THREE

My trip to Menen near the Belgian/French border was rather uneventful, though the Germans were omnipresent. I was somehow lucky enough to make contact with a local fellow who, for a nominal sum, took me across the border at night with his cache of contraband—black market cigarettes and ham.

From Lille, I took another train and, after traveling what seemed forever, arrived in Nice. Behold! I awoke to the sun and the sight of the most fantastic flowers. At night, the city's light shone brightly. In Antwerp, I had lived for two years where at night all the windows had to be covered so as not to let the slightest ray of light escape to the outside. As soon as I got to Nice, I went to the closest hotel and took a small room for a modest fee.

I stayed for about two weeks. Within a few days, I joined the underground and was given the job of putting anti-Fascist propaganda leaflets into mailboxes. One day, two Italian *carabinieri* came to the hotel and brought me to their headquarters where I met *Comandante* Riccone. The man looked immaculate. He bore a waxed mustache, its ends pointing undeniably upward. He wore a pistol; however, his was not as threatening to me because on many occasions I witnessed how Italian military personnel of all ranks ignored the solicited greetings from their so-called German allies. Those personal affronts comforted me, and I immediately knew where my loyalty would lie.

Comandante Riccone looked me up and down. After a moment, I let him know my feelings; my demeanor spoke volumes. The man had made a definite impression on me. Slowly, dramatically, he pushed his chair back from the table, rising and standing rigidly before me.

"What's your name, son?"

"Samuel Berlin," I replied.

A moment of silence followed. *Comandante* Riccone walked over to the window, put his hands behind his back, and slowly lifted himself up on his toes so that his boots made a crackling sound. With his back to me, he spoke.

"Mister Berlin, you will go tomorrow to Barcelonnette in the Alps with a pass, which I will give you, and there you'll wait until I arrive. You'll then present yourself to me for further instructions. There you will be considered under forced residence." Then he turned to me and said, "Better and safer with us than with them; right?"

"Yes, sir." I could see that he was pleased with my reply. I felt better because someone had made a decision for me. Indeed, I *did* feel safer with the Italians than with the Nazi Germans. An understatement, to be sure.

"The secretary at the exit will issue you the proper papers, which you'll present to me at the time of my arrival."

I stood looking at the fifty-five-year-old man of medium stature and pleasant face, suddenly realizing that he had finished what he had to say.

I said to him, "Thank you, my *Colonnéllo*," and noticed that he stretched slightly up on his toes, creating that undeniable crackling sound anew while still standing in place.

"It's *comandante*, not *colonnéllo*."

The *comandante's* correction, however, was an extremely weak protest. I left the room, and on my way out of headquarters was handed papers by a secretary who echoed Riccone's instructions that I had to present myself with the document at the *comandante's* office in Barcelonnette in the French Alps.

The next morning I boarded a bus at Place Massena in Nice. Toward the front of the bus, I took a window seat for the one-hundred-fifty-mile ride. That was a mistake because the bus followed narrow mountain roads and, more often than not, the road became virtually invisible. All I could see was downward. I was convinced that I would join the world of the hereafter. The bus swayed precariously, especially around the bends. For this I had to travel many miles only to tumble from some precipice?

I finally arrived at Barcelonnette around eight o'clock at night. I was completely caught by surprise because in Nice one could swim in the Mediterranean, but here there was only mud and snow. It was cold, and I had no warm clothing on or with me. I was shivering as I stood there for a while, watching the passengers hurriedly heading toward their destinations. *Which way now?* I thought. The bus had stopped at a small square with one impressive looking hotel. Above the entrance, I saw a sign: *Hotel des Alps*. No, I couldn't go there. It looked too expensive. The rest of the houses were small and unpretentious.

All I could see was one long, main street. I saw a gendarme standing next to his bicycle; he was looking directly at me. *Is he going to ride that thing in the mud?* I thought. *How could he?* Then I noticed that he was standing in front of a structure with a sign on which was painted, *Préfecture de Police.* I walked over to him, trying my best to circumvent the mud and puddles.

"*Mon Capitaine,*" I said, clearly noting the two medals on his chest rise two inches. I was learning and learning fast. "I'm looking for small, inexpensive lodging, and I wonder if you could direct me?" He chose not to correct my addressing him as a captain, and with exaggerated gestures, directed me to the Le Cheval Blanc, which was located about ten houses down the first side street. It had taken him a good two minutes of explaining. As I was about to leave, he asked, "What's your name?"

"Berlin. Samuel Berlin."

"Paul Piton. Sergeant Piton. Good night, Berlin."

"Good night, my Sergeant."

He touched his cap with his right hand, and I headed off to Le Cheval Blanc.

I enjoyed a decent supper and was shown to a room with a bed covered by a thick down-filled spread, the height of which practically reached my chin. A wash basin filled with water stood in a corner. A slanted window was located in the roof. I got undressed and started to cry again. I wiped my eyes and nose and decided then and there that unless I had a real good reason, I wasn't going to cry anymore. I uncovered the bed and lay down on a mattress that literally went from a three-foot height all the way down to the floor. I looked at myself lying there in the middle of this big bed, surrounded by a mound of mattress, a foot higher than my belly button. I laughed and laughed and played a silly game of trying to roll out of the bed, failing each and every time. I pushed, rolled back to the middle, and started gasping for air, laughing still harder until I was completely spent. Sometime later I fell asleep, and I slept well because I knew that no matter what happened I could never fall off this bed.

Upon awakening, I saw a big blue sky above me, and the sun was shining brightly. I climbed out of bed, washed and got dressed. The smell of inviting food reached my nostrils, and I was suddenly very hungry. I went downstairs and had coffee and real bread (not ersatz) with butter and jam. It was genuine bread without ground beans, along with the taste of true butter. I'd almost forgotten what real butter tasted like, for it had been two years. But then this was *la campagne*, the country, where there must be many farms.

I finished eating and decided to seek some sort of employment, but first a haircut. I walked to the main street, looking left then right. It was a rather long street with a few stores in the middle and several side streets, which I'd investigate later. I found a barber shop and walked in.

I sat and waited about two minutes. From behind a back curtain, a woman's voice told me to wait. I heard the sound of kitchen utensils. Finally, the curtain opened, and a pretty dark-haired young woman of about twenty-three came out and told me to take a seat in the barber chair. *A woman barber.* I felt uncomfortable.

"My name is Paulette. What's yours?" she asked.

"Sam Berlin."

"Pleased to meet you. Are you a tourist?"

"No, I'm a-a-a . . . I'm waiting for the Italian *comandante*."

Around my neck, Paulette placed a clean white sheet that covered my lap. She started snipping away, and her hands kept touching my face and neck.

"Why do you have to wait for the Italian

comandante?"

"Well, I'm considered a political threat, and I'm in forced residence. I must wait for him until he gets here."

Her feminine presence, so close yet so far, very much excited me. She smelled so good from some terribly delicious perfume.

"Where are you staying now?" she asked.

"At Le Cheval Blanc. I got here last night, and I'm looking for a job."

A clump of hair lodged itself between my ear and temple, and she blew it away. I felt terribly weak. As I looked down, I saw the contour of my manhood lifting the sheet that covered my lap. I felt very uncomfortable. My hands were wrapped tightly around the armrests of the chair. I didn't want to make any movement that might attract her attention to my physical discomfort.

"These are difficult and hard times for everyone," Paulette said.

"I know. And especially for me." *What was I saying? Not now, Sam. Not now.*

"Why don't you apply for a job at the Hotel des Alps. I'm sure you'll be able to find some employment."

"I think I'll do that as soon as you're finished with my hair."

"By the way," she said, "if you want to, we have a furnished room for rent, and it's much cheaper than what you're paying at Le Cheval Blanc."

"If it's *much* cheaper, I'll take it without looking at it."

Paulette finished cutting my hair and walked over to the sink. Wetting a clean towel, she came back and placed the cold cloth around my neck, then started wiping my neck and behind my ears.

"I believe a cold compress is sometimes better than a warm one in that it promotes blood circulation and calms the nerves."

I wondered if she realized what she had just said. My face turned crimson red.

Later, she showed me the room, which was on the third floor. In order to reach it, you could either go directly from the street or enter through a side door off the barber shop and through a large gated portal. One had to walk up a badly lit staircase. The room had a rickety bed made of copper, with a big ball on top of each post that stood approximately five feet high. Its headboard, comprised of ornate figure works, was also made from copper. A long wire hung from the ceiling with a scarred lampshade covering a small bulb, looking as though it might expire at any moment. A small sink with a half-rusted faucet stood in a corner. In order to liven up the dismal atmosphere, there was a brown faded photo of a soldier holding his rifle. An armoire completed the furnished room. I walked over to the solitary window, which was tall and narrow and faced a brick wall opposite the building.

I gave Paulette one month's rent in advance, telling her that I liked the room very much and that it would do fine. She seemed pleased that I expressed happiness over the room, telling me if I was in need of anything that I should let her know. If only she realized what she was saying.

I went to Le Cheval Blanc, gathered my belongings and brought them back to the room where I would spend the next eight months. I had been thinking in terms of only two or three months because over the BBC we learned that the Allies were making substantial military advances and that we would all surely be liberated from the *sale boche* (dirty krauts). But it was the middle of 1942, and we would all spend long nights and days before feeling safe again behind our respective doors.

I decided to investigate the town and learned that the whole village consisted of about twenty streets that abruptly ended in either fields or rock gullies. One could see mountains wherever one looked, and the air was usually crisp and invigorating. Unfortunately, the mountainous air also induced a hearty appetite, regrettable because food would become very scarce, especially when one hundred eighty political suspects arrived in Barcelonnette and took up residence. With the passing of time, food would rapidly become an extremely scarce commodity, even in the countryside. Ah, but I'm getting a bit ahead of myself.

I got a job as a general maintenance man and a dishwasher in the Hotel des Alps. The copper kettles were gigantic, and I had to wash them with ersatz soap. I might as well have used a rock.

Two weeks after my arrival in Barcelonnette, the Italian military personnel had set up their headquarters. I went to the *Préfecture de Police* and received instructions from *Comandante* Riccone.

"From now on, on a daily basis, you will present yourself to me and refer to yourself as 'Number One'. Once at ten o'clock in the morning and again at four o'clock in the afternoon. After that, you will proceed directly to where you live, and you'll not come out again for the entire evening."

Two *carabinieri* were standing next to Riccone, one of whom had red hair, blue eyes and stood six-foot-two, a rather sympathetic-looking fellow. For a moment we stared at each other, and I saw a warm glow emanating from his face. I smiled ever so unobtrusively, and to my delight saw him respond in kind. I sensed that I had a friend in him.

"You may go now," I heard the *comandante* say to me.

As I walked out to the street, a man of about twenty-five years old, with a head of beautiful wavy hair, tried to pass me while I was trying to pass him. However, when he moved to the right, I moved left and we simultaneously reversed our movements. He finally grabbed me by the shoulders and said, "You move left, and I'll move left; otherwise, we'll be dancing around here till tomorrow." I liked the way he kidded and spoke to me. "By the way, did you see the *comandante* just now?"

"Yes, I did."

"What kind of guy is he?"

"Oh, he's really okay; not like the *boche*. He's got humanity about him. He's assigned a job to do, that's all."

"My name is Moise Behar."

"Mine is Sam Berlin."

We shook hands.

"Good to meet you, Sam. Are you here with someone?"

"No, I'm all alone. How about you, Moise?"

"I'm here with my brother, his wife and their two little children. Why don't I go see the *comandante*, and we'll have a chat later on; okay?"

"Fine. I'll see you later."

I went back to my copper kettles at the hotel.

One afternoon, on the way to my room, I saw the two *carabinieri* with short-barreled rifles slung over their shoulders. They were walking slowly in step, just outside of town. As they approached, the redhead from *Comandante* Riccone's office struck up a conversation with me, and I learned that the soldier was born in Sicily. His name was Romeo, and his French was good enough so that he could express himself fairly well. I did not let on that I could speak Italian. His colleague didn't seem to care for any conversation, yet seemed interested in what we had to say.

"Do you smoke, Sam?" Romeo asked.

"Yes," I replied, "but you can't get any cigarettes these days."

Romeo retrieved a pack of militia cigarettes and offered me one. As I took it, he said, "Take another."

The other *carabinieri* looked sideways at his companion.

"Go on, take another one," Romeo repeated.

I did and thanked him. We continued our separate ways.

CHAPTER FOUR

Each time I went to get a haircut, I looked forward to seeing Paulette. One day I met her at the entrance to the house. She must have noticed something wrong because she asked me, "What's the matter, Sam? Are you all right?"

I bluntly stated, "No."

"Well, what is it?"

I replied, "I'm lonely."

We stared at each other for a while before she took hold of my hand and led me behind the door. After a moment, she asked, "Would you like me to kiss you?"

My heart leaped to my Adam's apple, and, without waiting for a reply, she put her arms around me and kissed my lips fully with a passion that left me dizzy. Just as abruptly, she said, "*Mon cher*, Sam. I must go now. *Au revoir.*"

Finally, I had a girlfriend. I felt wonderful. I was drunk with passion. I wanted to shout—to sing. I was so in love. My first girlfriend! I was eighteen. I would work at the hotel as a cleaning boy, as a cook's helper . . . whatever. I would take a job at night doing *anything.* I was going to provide for the both of us so that she wouldn't have to cut hair anymore. She'd be my woman, and I'd be her man. *Sam, you lucky son of a gun.*

That night I slept very restlessly. In the morning, I went to the hotel, and in passing the barber shop, I saw Paulette and waved to her. She responded with puckered lips. *You've got it made,* I sang to myself and continued jubilantly to my job when I saw Moise.

"Good morning, Moise. How are you?" I greeted.

"I'm fine, Sam. What's with you? You look as if you're going to be liberated soon."

"You're right, Moise. I'm in love."

"Oh, really. And who's the lucky girl, may I ask?"

"Paulette. We're in love."

Moise looked at me strangely and smiled. "Oh, that's nice," he said flatly.

I didn't understand his attitude.

"Hey, listen, Sam. You know the Zimmermans?

"Sure I do."

"Well, you know they have a daughter whom I'm fond of, and her father loves to play cards. Why don't you and I go over there tonight and have a game of belote with her father."

"But you know that we can't be out after dark."

"Oh, come on. What will they do to us if they catch us?"

"I don't know," I said, "but I think that we'd be taking an unnecessary chance."

"Don't worry. They won't catch us. We'll be careful."

I hesitated a moment, then agreed. We had made arrangements to meet at a predetermined location at eight o'clock that evening.

There was a full moon. I left my place at ten minutes to eight and made myself as unobtrusive as possible by walking very close to the houses. Moise was waiting at an open hallway near where the Zimmermans lived.

"You see? There's nothing to it, is there?"

I wondered if he could hear the pounding of my heart. "Yes, it was nothing," I acceded with feigned assurance.

We enjoyed a lovely evening playing cards, Moise more interested in rubbing knees with Zimmerman's daughter, Clara. We decided to leave at eleven o'clock.

We said good-night, walked out to the abandoned street, and cautiously started home. Suddenly, we heard footsteps coming toward us, so we quickly ducked into a doorway, shrinking into its shadows. The sounds became louder and louder as we moved furtively within the enclosed space. We knew that the footsteps belonged to the *carabinieri*, walking in unison, side by side, patrolling the streets. Moise, his voice heavy with tension, whispered into my ear.

"Turn your back to the street and put your arms around me. In the darkness, they may take us for lovers and ignore us."

We wrapped our arms around each other, and Moise put his head upon my chest. We waited anxiously. The sound of footsteps stopped in front of the doorway. A flashlight flickered, its beam dancing upon the walls. We did not move an inch. The light shone upon us then disappeared. The sound of footsteps continued down the street. We released one another and began to breathe easily.

"Do you think they bought that act?" I asked.

"Well, they chose to ignore us," Moise replied, "which means they didn't know the score. Yes?"

"Yes, but I feel very uncomfortable."

"Don't worry, Sam. You'll see that everything is going to be all right."

We bid each other good-night, and I proceeded to walk home, clinging close to the houses on the shadowy side of the street. When I arrived home and was about to enter the building, I noticed a faint light coming from the barber shop. I found it odd that someone would be in the shop at this late hour. I took hold of the handle and slowly opened the door. What I saw jarred me so that I almost cried out. On the barber chair sat Sergeant Piton and Paulette, both of them completely undressed and in a very compromising position. I left the door ajar and proceeded to walk upstairs to my room. I was bitterly broken within. I undressed to go to bed, and as I was about to switch off the light, I looked at the picture of the soldier on the wall and said aloud, "I hope you croak, you son of a bitch." It took me forever to fall asleep.

The next morning my eyes snapped open like the aperture of a camera. I was instantly awake in spite of having tossed about all night, having even gotten up once in order to turn the face of the soldier flush to the wall, which really didn't help much.

My thoughts returned to last night's encounter with the *carabinieri*. I had to report to the *comandante* this morning. What'll happen? Had the soldiers recognized me? Maybe they didn't even see us. Maybe they had. All sorts of scenarios were running through my mind. How I wished I didn't have to report.

I went to the hotel and had something to eat. Breakfast was anything but elaborate, usually consisting of some nondescript baked mass and black liquid. This morning, however, the chef gave me a freshly baked croissant. Was this a bad omen . . . like a prisoner's last meal? When was the ax going to come down on me? What was there to live for, now, anyway? Life was getting complicated and confusing. Maybe I should go back on the bus and jump from one of the cliffs.

It was five minutes to ten. With a thumping heart, I walked up to the *comandante's* office. There were about twenty people in front of me. The secretary was taking the roll call. As I entered the room, I saw Romeo with his partner standing next to the *comandante*. Romeo looked at me and imperceptibly lifted his shoulders in a gesture of helplessness. That's when I started perspiring cold sweat. There were two people in front of me, identified as fifty-two and seventeen. I called out, "One." The *comandante* slowly and deliberately stretched out his right arm, gesturing me aside. People behind me continued calling out their numbers. Finally, it appeared that no one else was coming.

The *comandante* leaned back in his chair and stared at me like a predator contemplating its prey. He seemed to enjoy the moment, extending it, choosing to say nothing. Finally, he stood then sat on the edge of the table. He retrieved and lit a cigarette. A big billow of smoke mixed with some of his sweet-smelling cologne reached me.

"Who was the woman you were with last night, Mr. Berlin?"

I wanted to go to the bathroom, badly. I said nothing.

"It won't help any if you withhold information, which could be of utmost importance."

I wanted to go to the bathroom and lay down. Something was wrong with my knees. I finally managed to unglue my tongue from my palate and said, "I am a gentleman and cannot divulge the name of the lady."

"*Le nom,*" he half sang and shouted to me. The pitch was perfect for his vocal range.

"I'm sorry, *Comandante.* Even if I have to die for it, I'll never divulge the name of the lady." *What the hell was I saying!*

Romeo stood there expressionless, but the color of his face practically matched the color of his hair.

"Then I have no choice but to pass sentence on you."

I wanted to throw up. He walked over to the window, put his hands behind his back, then stretched upward on his toes; the sound of crackling boots seemed deafening.

"I hereby sentence you to four months house arrest. You'll not go out of your house till I send for you. Food will be provided to you once a day, and the only way to en your sentence, is to tell me the name of the woman. You may go now. Oh, by the way, should you decide to go out during the time of your sentence, you'll spend one year in prison. Now, you may go."

I shot a glance to Romeo and quickly left. I walked

over to the hotel and told those who needed to know what had happened. They felt most indignant about the harsh sentence I received; they were very complimentary toward my noble behavior for not divulging the name of the *woman*. I went to my room knowing full well that this was going to be a very unpleasant experience, suddenly realizing that one of the most precious aspects of life is freedom—freedom worth fighting for. I was to mature rapidly in the months to follow.

That evening, someone knocked at the door. It was Romeo, and behind him stood my friend, Moise. Romeo had a pot of pasta and beans for me. He looked very embarrassed.

"I'm sorry, Sam," he said. "I couldn't do anything else because I was on patrol with sourpuss, and knowing him the way I do, there was just no way out."

I told him to forget it because I understood perfectly well. Moise expressed his admiration for me and promised to visit often. I spent the next three weeks in my room or roaming the house up to the threshold. Paulette came to see me a couple of times, but she couldn't understand why I didn't love her anymore, and I didn't tell her. I asked her to do me a favor, which was to let me know the very moment the *comandante* was having his hair cut. A few days later Romeo came with some food and information.

"Sam," he said, "my girl, that is, I mean, Paulette, said to tell you that the *comandante* is having his hair cut, right now."

Well, it appeared that Paulette liked uniforms. I didn't. After Romeo left, I ran downstairs and saw the *comandante* sitting smugly in the barber chair. Paulette was powdering his neck rather enthusiastically. That barber chair never seemed to grow cold. Comandante Riccone stood, straightened his uniform, pivoted left then right before a mirror, making sure that his appearance, from head to toe, was perfect. He exited the side door where I was standing but said nothing to me. He stopped at the edge of the hallway where it met the sidewalk, withdrawing a cigarette.

I thought to address him as 'my lordship,' 'your gracious highness,' but instead I said, "My dear *Generale*." He looked at me with disdain. "I'm suffering so," I continued. "I'm so young and full of life and your Graciousness is in a position to relieve me from this terrible punishment." I heard the sound of his boots creaking. *Go, go, Sam. You're hitting home.* He said nothing and kept smoking. "You know, I could be your son and you my father, and I don't believe, being of your flesh and having your blood flowing in my veins would you have the heart to see me suffer like this." *Say something, you son of a bitch. I'm running out of words.* I grabbed his hand and held it in mine. "I'm pleading for my freedom, and the hand that I hold has the power to liberate me, allowing me to walk the streets and breathe again."

He wrestled his hand free from mine and, lo and behold, stretched his hand toward the street, stating, "I liberate you."

"Oh, thank you, my—"

"But on one condition, Samuel. Don't ever go out after curfew."

"I promise you that I won't."

Without saying another word, he walked away. At the same time, Paulette came out of the shop.

"My goodness, Sam. You handled him beautifully. I wish that I had the talent to handle people like you just did."

"From the way I've seen how you handle Sergeant Piton, you don't need any lessons from me," I declared.

CHAPTER FIVE

The weeks ran into months, and I thought I'd never get out of this place. Finally, one day, as I walked to the hotel, Romeo came out from the *Préfecture de Police*, and as he saw me, he hurried over.

"Sam, for us it's over. We're going home."

"What do you mean it's over?"

"We've capitulated and are no more allied with the Germans."

"Thank God!" I welcomed those words.

"*Comandante* Riccone has asked me to spread the word among the political detainees that we're crossing over the Alps into Italy, and whoever wants to join us, can."

"I'm going with you," I said.

"Fine," he replied. "We're going by bus to a point

near the border and then crossing over by foot."

I was looking forward to the trip. It felt as though a tremendous load had been lifted off my shoulders. I was free—or was I? Anyway, it was a good feeling, even though we knew that the Germans were still at war. We didn't know where they were situated because our area of France was under the jurisdiction of the Italians. Now that Italy had laid down its arms, exactly where the Germans were positioned became the big question. I made up my mind then and there that I would head southward until I made contact with the Americans.

The chef at the hotel had given me some provisions, among which was a rather large sausage that I would guard very closely and eat only when I was sure that no one was watching. The buses arrived, and we departed, traveling to a point where the mountains abruptly became steep. Forming a snake-like line, we walked over hill and dale. My friend Moise and his brother carried the two children. I felt so sorry for everyone in the same predicament of having to carry and care for their children.

Romeo and the other *carabinieri* still wore their uniforms. *Comandante* Riccone was wearing civilian clothes. At one point, he came over to me.

"Sam. You understand that I had a job to do. I had

to maintain my position, especially in front of my men."

"I understand," I replied.

"Don't hesitate to come and visit me after the war. I have a son your age and a wife who cooks magical dishes. I have a vineyard with grapes that are as big as plums, and you'll be treated as one of the family. You have the eyes of my boy and remind me of him every time I see you."

Riccone was obviously moved, and so was I. He put his hand out to me and said, "Good-bye my boy, and walk with God." The man turned abruptly, walking ahead of me, disappearing somewhere up front with the others.

At dusk, we arrived in Valdieri, which was the first town on Italian soil. I had blisters on my feet and was grateful to find some rest in an abandoned army barrack. Moise was lying on an old mattress next to me when he asked what I planned to do. I told him of my intention to proceed south and join the Americans. Moise said he would remain in Valdieri. I told him that it was not such a good idea since we didn't know where the Germans were.

We all slept soundly that night. Upon awakening, I thought that my feet were on fire. Yesterday's march up and over the mountains was one long trek. I took my shoes and socks off and saw an ugly sight: two blistering feet, one of which had a bleeding puncture wound from a nail in my shoe. We had no medication with us. Those who carried medical supplies had moved on ahead.

I set my physical concern aside. All in all, I was a free agent—at least for the moment. I allowed myself the luxury of entertaining all kinds of plans, one of which was most definite. I would head southward to meet up with the Americans. That was my primary concern. I wanted to see and meet the kinds of people who I only saw in the cinema: Tom Mix and other cowboys who always defeated the savage Indians. Even Rin-Tin-Tin, who thought like a human. Yes, the Americans, whose marksmanship was unerring, being with either pistol or rifle, putting down vile perpetrators. The Americans were my heroes . . . always just and kind . . . the movie concluding with a cowboy strumming his guitar before a setting sun.

I pulled on what was left of those socks, put on my shoes, painfully stood, picked up my worn valise and carefully stepped over sleeping bodies, moving toward Moise. I gently nudged him by the shoulder.

"Hey, Sam. What are you doing up so early?"

"I'm heading southward, now. I want to meet the Americans, and I would like very much for you to come with me."

"I wish that I could come with you, but I cannot," Moise replied. "Who's going to help my brother with the children?"

"Well, Moise. I've made up my mind. I'm going to Cuneo and take the train to Rome; or I'll walk, swim or crawl, but I'm going."

"Go in peace with God's protection," Moise said.

We shook hands, and I walked back over the sleeping bodies of men, women and children, leaving the barrack to meet the Americans.

CHAPTER SIX

Part of my journey to Cuneo was in a farmer's cart, drawn by a donkey; next, came a short but blissful car ride. No Germans were in sight, and I was hoping that it was the end of the war. Little did I know how those termites were going to spread and rot the foundation of humanity. I arrived at the station in Cuneo, where I witnessed sheer bedlam. A train would be leaving for Rome, shortly. It was packed mainly with Italians, some dressed in civilian clothing, some in military uniforms. I was limping badly and had to get on this train to rest my feet and weary body.

I studied the situation and decided to get on the train without buying a ticket since there was practically no supervision and would probably prove catch-as-catch-can anyhow. I hobbled over to an open train window where a man was talking in harsh terms with someone on the platform who wanted to board the train.

"No more room," the man emphatically said to the other below him.

I limped closer to the man hanging out the window, and as he saw me standing there, he spoke to his friend whose body also half-protruded from the opening. One of them pointed to me and waved me even closer. When I was in reach, they both grabbed my arms and lifted me into the train, along with my valise. One of them asked me if I was wounded. I didn't catch on at first. He pointed to my leg. I invented a story on the spot.

"A German shot me in my leg, and I am going to join my newlywed Italian wife in Rome."

I will never know how they found room for me aboard that over-packed train. There were shoulder-to-shoulder Italian soldiers everywhere, lying in luggage racks and on the floor. One man, looking pallid and exhausted, was sitting on a toilet seat. I finally realized that if I were to have any rest at all, I would have to squeeze myself beneath the seat where five soldiers were sitting in a space meant for four.

Explaining and expanding on my tall tale, I had asked one of those soldiers to make room for me by lifting his feet so that I could squeeze under their seat.

Impressed by my story, he immediately asked the others to make room for a wounded soldier with a big bullet hole in *each* leg. They responded in unison, and I squeezed under the seat. The floor was covered in dust, dirt and strewn with wrappers and discarded apple cores. I didn't care because after a few minutes I was sound asleep.

I woke up as the train jarred into motion. We all had one thing in common: we all wanted to go home. Moments later, I fell back to sleep. I don't know how long I slept, but I was suddenly awakened anew by shooting.

"*Aufhalten!*" a German soldier shouted.

"Let's run for it!" someone from our compartment yelled.

It seemed like everyone wanted to jump out of the windows at the same time, and in a matter of seconds, the compartment was emptied except for four men and me. The train had stopped in a small town, and men were running all over the tracks. To my horror I saw three bodies sprawled in unnatural positions across the tracks. The shooting continued. From a distance, I could distinctly hear a German shouting.

"*Dokumente.*"

I was really frightened. I withdrew some papers

from my coat pocket, one of which permitted me to stay in France on a transient basis; of course, it was no good here. My birth certificate and Belgian identification were no good either because across the face of them was the word JEW, written in red. Next, I unfolded my diploma, stating that I had graduated with honors as a tool and die maker from the trade school in Antwerp. It was an impressive document. Two imposing-looking lions stood on their hind legs, facing one another, a large red shield separating them, clawing at its respective sides. At the bottom were several official stamps from the City of Antwerp, along with signatures from several school dignitaries.

A pen; I needed a pen. One of the men had one, and I asked him if I could borrow it for a moment. Along with the use of a discarded matchbook, I immediately proceeded to draw a stubby heavy cross in the center of the red shield. I succeeded in making the edges very straight, with arms of equal length set at right angles. I continued working, forming the emblem with bold strokes of ink. The shouts were coming closer.

"*Dokumente.*"

Shouts mixed with screams. I finished my drawing and returned the pen to the man. It was obvious we were all very nervous. The shooting continued, and I was feeling very weak. I leaned back and closed my eyes, summoning up all the strength I had left in me. At the door to the compartment stood two German soldiers with rifles at the ready, flanking a man wearing a long leather coat.

"*Dokumente*," the German officer demanded as he reached out with his right hand.

Every one of us had different identification. The officer took hold of a paper from the man seated closest to him, scrutinized the document then returned it. His eyes darted from one document to the next. As he cast his eyes upon my paper, I felt as if he was going to order one of the soldiers to shoot me on the spot. After what seemed like an eternity, he finished examining my diploma, handed it back, perused the papers of others then ordered his men to move on to the next compartment.

"*Dokumente*," I heard him bark.

I closed my eyes and thanked the Almighty for His protection. Upon opening them, I looked at the swastika which I had drawn. I was exhilarated that my plan had succeeded. The fellow asked me what kind of paper I had shown. It looked so impressive. When I told him what it was, he gave me a friendly tap on the shoulder and said,

"Bravissimo!" I asked him what kind of paper he had presented. The man showed me a piece of paper declaring that he had been released from the hospital after having been treated for gonorrhea. We remained at the station for hours before finally moving southward again.

The following morning we arrived in Rome and saw Germans crawling all over the place. I walked briskly out into the street as if I knew exactly where I was going. *Where to now?* I wondered. *Keep on going. Don't linger. Just move on,* I told myself. I didn't know whether to go left or right. Seemingly, with purpose of mind, I crossed the street then made alternate turns. In actuality, I was wandering aimlessly. I saw a street sign, *Piazza di Indipendènza.* I looked around and saw a hotel sign: *Albèrgo Lalus.* It looked expensive. My feet were killing me; I limped badly. I walked into the lobby and saw a few lounges and chairs. I so badly wanted to sit down, directing myself toward one of the seats. I passed a large mirror on the wall. I looked at myself and was shocked. I looked filthy and disheveled and bore deep black rings under my eyes. I plopped down in one of the seats. I was beside myself. I sat there for a good quarter hour before a man approached, sitting down next to me. The hair on my neck rose.

"Looks like you had a long trip."

"*Sì,*" I replied.

"Are you going to stay here?"

"*Sì.*"

"Any family?"

"No."

"Are you meeting anyone?"

"No, no one."

"You are not Italian, are you?"

Now, I was caught for sure. Could I pull off another coupe as I had with the diploma document ploy? I felt my heart sinking.

"Don't be afraid," he said. "I'm a friend."

I looked at him in bewilderment.

"Are you a refugee?" he questioned.

"Yes," I replied.

"You look as if you are on the run. Right?"

"Yes."

"Okay. I'll lay it out bluntly for you. I'm in charge of recruiting people for a clandestine group dedicated to fighting the Germans. Are you interested in joining?"

I didn't say a thing.

"Have you any money?"

I shook my head

He put his hand in a pocket and retrieved a bunch of Italian lira. "This will help you for a while. You'll take a room here, wash up, and I will contact you tomorrow."

He took my valise and walked over to the front desk with me. "A room for Mister Antonio Bruno," he said.

I was given a key while I signed in as Antonio Bruno. He shook my hand and introduced himself as *Signore* Gribante—captain of Italian Intelligence.

I walked up one flight to my room and was grateful to see that in case of an emergency, I could make a quick escape from a window, onto a ledge, down to an alley and onto a side street.

I took a blissful warm bath with ersatz soap that did not foam. Finally, after having dried myself, I walked over to the bed. It stood high off the floor, reminiscent of the bed I slept in at Le Cheval Blanc. I immediately crawled into bed and could not help but smile.

CHAPTER SEVEN

The next morning I heard a knock at my door. I tensed.

"Gribante."

Recognizing the voice, I relaxed. I got out of bed and let the captain in.

"How do you feel, Antonio?"

"Fine, Captain," I replied.

"From now on it's Mister Gribante," he said.

He sat down on the bed, studied me for a moment before handing me a green identification card stamped with a swastika.

"This will identify you as Antonio Bruno, born in Naples and living at Via di Fiori. You are officially recorded in that municipality, so try to improve your Italian. You may be able to fool the Germans with your

Italian vocabulary, but you won't get away with it if you're caught by the Fascisti." He withdrew a pistol from his pocket and handed it to me. "This is a fully-loaded weapon. Have you had any experience with firearms?"

I told him the only experience I had was shooting air guns and rifles at the local fairs in Antwerp, and that I was fairly accurate with both.

Next, he gave me food coupons. Pausing for a moment, the man looked down at my feet. Without looking up, he asked, "Would you hesitate to shoot a German?"

Without faltering, I answered, "No."

Gribante seemed pleased with my prompt answer. He asked about my background. After I told him what had happened to my family and me, he seemed saddened yet satisfied.

Captain Gribante got up. "I'll be in touch with you in a couple of days. Stick around the hotel and remember that this is not an air gun you are carrying." He told me to see the doctor next-door for my blisters and to tell him that Gribante had sent me.

After he left, I limped downstairs and went to see the doctor. The man cleaned my blisters and put salve and bandages on them. When I told him who had sent me, the doctor refused to take any money. He asked if I had other shoes because the ones I wore were badly shredded. They were the only pair I had. He disappeared for a moment, then returned with a pair of sturdy-looking boots in hand.

"Here, try these on."

They fit perfectly, and I was grateful to receive them.

"I am an amateur mountain climber," he said, "and although you are in the city, these boots are practically indestructible."

Again, I offered the doctor money, but he refused payment.

"I know your connection with the captain, so let me give you something else." He filled a small box with bandages and different kinds of ointments. "You probably won't have to use these, but just in case, take them with you."

I thanked him profusely and left with my well-fitting mountain climbing boots. I put away the box of bandages and salves in my room and went down to see if I could find something to eat. As I entered the lobby, a woman of about forty looked me over before approaching. She wore an ill-fitting housedress and walked with a bad limp.

"What are you looking for, *caro*?"

I told her I was looking to buy some groceries.

"Why don't you come upstairs with me and I'll make you something to eat, and then we'll play a little. Do you have some money?"

"Yes."

"Good, then come upstairs with me."

I was impressed by the generosity of these people, but I wondered what she meant by *playing*. She must have meant card playing or dominoes. I'd find out soon enough.

We walked up a couple of flights, and I followed her into a room that was much larger than mine. A big bed and a washstand were set against a wall; a table and chairs stood at the foot of the bed.

"You want to eat first or play?"

That was a funny thing to ask, but since I was curious, I chose to *play* first. With that, she told me to take off my boots and pants—and then I understood perfectly. I was finally going to be initiated. I took off my clothing and was timidly aroused. As I got into bed with a pounding heart, I couldn't believe what I saw. She was undressed and was in the process of taking off her artificial leg. I was so shocked that I started losing my, ah . . . excitement. As she moved close to me, the door opened and two men in heated conversation came into the room and sat down at the table at the foot of the bed. One was scolding the other for not having bought one hundred kilos of spaghetti on the black market, since it was such a bargain. The other defended his action by insisting he had done the right thing. The woman interrupted by telling the men that she had a visitor. They suddenly stopped arguing and looked at us.

"What's your name, *bellezza*?"

"Antonio," I replied.

"Meet my two cousins," the woman said.

One man had an ordinary look about him. The other had hair that looked like black ice. He bore a pencil-thin moustache and wore a red carnation in the lapel of his black pinstriped suit. They both stood up and came over to me, extending their hands in greeting.

"Marco," the ordinary-looking man said as I shook his hand.

"Poppo," the Moustache Pete said, giving me a big smile. "Poppo Piacere."

"Antonio Bruno," I said, shaking his hand.

Suddenly, they both turned around and continued their argument while the woman propped herself up on her elbows and joined the men in their dispute. There was something very wrong here. Clumsily, the woman got up and moved to the foot of the bed, joining the two men in a now vociferous dialogue. I decided that I didn't want to *play* anymore and got dressed while they were arguing away.

One flight down and I could still hear them yelling.

I found a small grocery store and bought some provisions with my food coupons. There were Germans all over the place, but with my new identification papers, I felt secure.

I stuck close to the hotel for a couple of days when Captain Gribante came to visit me.

"We're going to have a meeting" he said, "in the catacombs, and you should be there tomorrow evening with all your personal belongings."

The following evening, I packed up everything and walked downstairs. I saw the woman I met the other day, and she asked me if I wanted to *play* again. I declined, thanked her and continued my way to the catacombs.

There, I met the captain and about twenty other men. Among them was one fellow who had a pistol in his belt. The barrel almost reached his kneecap. I didn't know if he was very short or the barrel was very long. I came to the conclusion that he was very short and his pistol was a portable cannon. From the captain we learned that the Germans had started raiding a few hotels. Therefore, our group had to stay in the catacombs until we received orders from the upper echelon.

The living conditions were almost subhuman. We had little light, and it was very depressing. There wasn't enough food, which added to our woes. We stayed there for a week before being told that a carpenter's shop near St. Peter's Cathedral was available to us. We moved in, and conditions improved immediately. At least we didn't have to behave like moles.

One day I walked in the street and spied a truck parked at the curb. The back of the vehicle was filled with German black bread. A soldier was sitting on top of the loaves. As I moved closer, I saw a woman approaching the truck. The soldier and the woman looked at one another. Suddenly, she grabbed for a loaf of bread. The soldier had anticipated her move, raised his rifle and fired a bullet into her chest. She dropped to the ground with the loaf of bread lying next to her. I was terribly shaken by the incident. People scattered into the doorways, and for a moment there was absolute silence in the street. Men and women were watching from behind their sheltered positions. I was inflamed and knew what I had to do, regardless of the consequences. I stepped into a doorway and retrieved my pistol from under my coat and beneath my belt, putting the weapon in an outer pocket. I stepped out of the doorway and walked toward the soldier who was staring down at the dead woman. He looked at me, then back at the woman. I could see that the rifle was next to him. I withdrew my hand from my coat pocket, pointed the pistol at the soldier, and squeezed the trigger. The bullet found its mark somewhere in the man's chest. He dropped instantly. As the soldier lay there dying, I heard him mutter, "Ma, Ma."

Suddenly, there came a roar of bravos and bravissimos from the people, running out from everywhere, storming the truck and emptying it of the loaves of bread in no time flat. I ran back to our hideaway at the carpenter's shop.

Captain Gribante learned of the incident, and I was

congratulated by everyone for my deed. However, I felt sick because of the loss of two lives over a loaf of bread.

One night a couple of refugees seeking shelter came to our hideaway. I recognized them from Barcelonnette. They told us that the Germans had the town of Valdieri surrounded and that most of the people had been transported to Auschwitz. They did not take my friend Moise because he broke his own legs by tying a rope around a heavy case, lifting it from a height high above him before releasing the weight upon his outstretched limbs.

The following day I was riding on a bus near the Coliseum when someone shouted, "Raid!" The Germans were rounding up people, shipping them off to forced labor camps. I felt that every German soldier was looking for me in view of what I had done recently. I didn't relish the thought of having killed someone, and the rationale that I did so because the soldier shot the woman over a loaf of bread didn't help any. Paradoxically, I felt that the next time might be easier, and I started questioning that very dilemma. I wrestled with the fact that within every uniform was a living person.

My first thought was to get out of that bus. Fortunately, it was not too crowded, and in no time, I was on the street. I sized the situation up quickly. Both sides of the street were barricaded, and there was no way out. I took a few running steps and entered a small building. I ran up four or five flights of stairs and knocked on a door. I was breathing very heavily. A middle-aged woman opened the door.

"The Germans are making a raid, and I am in need of help. Please hide me."

She let me in. A young woman was lying on a big bed. Next to her, on a night table, were medicine bottles. *Where to hide?* The closet was too small. The kitchen had no hiding place. And then, in desperation, I blurted out, "Let me go into bed with your daughter, please."

For a moment the woman looked at me aghast.

"I'll lie under the mattress. Please, in the name of God!"

We heard crashing noises and loud banging downstairs.

"Quickly," she said, "get under."

Together, we lifted the big mattress halfway, and I lay down upon the bedsprings. The mother lowered the mattress on top of me, and the daughter positioned half her body above mine. With my face to one side, I managed to retrieve my pistol, holding my hand alongside my body. I silently said two prayers: one, that the Germans wouldn't catch me; secondly, that I shouldn't first suffocate. Although there was really plenty of air, I started feeling claustrophobic. Perspiration was pouring from every pore in my body. The mattress with the woman's weight upon me left me gasping. I was in a physical predicament. I wanted to get out from there badly.

After a moment that seemed forever, I heard the Germans ascending the stairs. Then came a banging on the door.

"*Un momento*," the mother said.

The door opened.

"Who lives here?" a soldier demanded.

"Just me and my daughter."

"Mama, mama, I can't breathe!" The daughter coughed loudly.

"What is wrong with her?"

"My poor baby; she is so sick. I don't know what to do for her. She suffers from a dangerous and contagious disease. She has typhus. Not even the doctor will come up. He sends medicine. Please help me move her and the bed to the other room. There is a window there. Perhaps she can breathe better."

My God, I thought. If they discovered me, at least one of them was going to die. I could barely breathe. I felt as though my chest was caving. My neck was aching. *God, help me to hold out just a little longer.* I heard their boots stomping away from the bed. I heard them leave. I almost threw the woman off me. I landed on my hands and knees, gasping for air. Thank God. I got lucky again. But was it true? Was the girl contagious?

The woman helped me up and gave me a glass of water then asked me to put away my pistol, which I did. I did not want to endanger these noble people with my presence and was about to leave. I asked her if her daughter was really contagious.

"Yes," she said.

I stiffened.

"She has a very bad cold," she said with a sly smile.

She grabbed my hand and kissed my forehead; her expression suddenly changed. "The German soldiers took my son. Go with God."

My mother's face came into mind.

I left my two saviors and waited in the hallways for a few hours just to make sure the Germans had finished their raid. Finally, I left the building and returned to the carpenter's shop.

Captain Gribante told me the Allies were advancing in southern Italy, and that we should soon be liberated. I waited four weeks in a state of great apprehension before deciding to head south. I told the captain of my plans, and he understood my feelings. I wanted to return the pistol, but he said that I should keep it and use it when needed, being sure to make a hasty retreat he added with a grin.

I said good-bye to the captain and the group of men, picked up my meager belongings and left Rome, heading southward to meet my liberators—the Americans. I didn't use public transportation. I marched. The boots the doctor had given me felt good.

Soon, I was in the countryside. I stopped at a small farm and asked the family for some water. In the course of our conversation, I learned that the war was still continuing to the east.

I headed in an easterly direction toward Abruzzi. It was rough walking. By nightfall, I came to another farm and sought shelter. The only place they had for me was in the barn. I slept on dry hay and was eaten up alive by fleas. They crept into my trousers and chewed heartily away. They were jumping in such great numbers that they made a sort of humming noise. It was an awful experience. I left early in the morning. Every time I had asked where the front lines were, a farmer pointed to the mountains and said, "On the other side." One mountain after another. My same question. Their same answer.

As I traveled, I ate what was available en route. Sometimes I was lucky and fed a good meal by folks who cared. Other times I had to spend the night with an empty stomach, for food was often scarce. Some of the farmers made bread from crushed corn that seemed as heavy as lead. Others made polenta, which was boiled cornmeal. They spread the crushed mass on a wooden board, topped with a mixture of boiled sausages, olive oil and other ingredients. Everybody would gather around the table with a fork and help themselves. I quickly discovered that this kind of eating left me with terrible stomach pains, and I sometimes debated with myself if it would perhaps be better to forgo the corn bread or polenta instead of being racked with stomach pains. Hunger usually proved the motivating factor, shortly followed by pain.

The families played a game called morra, in which two participants call out a number not exceeding ten, simultaneously extending zero to five fingers. If the total number of fingers matched the number called by a player, that person received a point. You needed five points to win the round. The game is then repeated with other family members and friends. When all but two players are eliminated, the one with the highest score is declared the winner—the *patròno*. The runner-up is the *satto patròno*. The *patròno* takes command of a bottle of wine and could drink the whole bottle if he so wished. The *satto patròno* could make suggestions to the *patròno* as to whom he might offer a glass of wine, which the *patròno* could refuse. However, in the end, everybody received a glass of wine. When the bottle of wine was empty, another was brought to the table, the game repeated, resulting in an elevated spirit of humor and intoxication.

One evening, I could hear artillery fire in the distance and see the flashing light reflecting beneath a cloudy firmament. *It'll all be over soon*, I told myself. *Then you're going to celebrate by having a royal meal followed with a sweet creamy cake topped with lovely frosting. You'll find yourself a woman and know what the good life is all about.* As I stood there looking at the darting flashes reflected in the low clouds, I made this vow, which I intended to keep. Adjusting the pistol in my breast pocket, I came back to reality. For a brief moment my spirits had soared. I gathered the collar of the coat about my neck and went to sleep with fleas.

CHAPTER EIGHT

The next day I learned that the Allies were at Cassino. I was near the town of Sora, about forty kilometers to the north of Cassino. I decided to head in the general direction of the fighting, walking along narrow paths that snaked through the mountains, avoiding main roads where the presence of German soldiers was sure to be prevalent.

One night, I found myself in a wild and remote area. The wind was whipping through the mountains. It was cold because the elevation was approximately five to six thousand feet. I was desperately looking for shelter, and I finally came upon a low shed that was built to house sheep as indicated by the droppings within. I was so cold that I had to make a fire, which I had no difficulty starting. There was plenty of wood. After awhile, half my body was warm, the other half freezing. In order to stay warm, I had to turn constantly. The coat I wore was inadequate.

I remained in the shed for about an hour when I was suddenly joined by five Italian soldiers who had seen the light of the fire through the ill-fitting slats. The five had escaped from German camps and were heading home. Later that evening, a sixth man appeared. A strange sight he was, framed there in the firelight. He had black curly hair and a handsome Mediterranean face. He wore tattered clothes and was smiling broadly, exhibiting perfect white teeth.

"Can I join you people for some warmth?"

We welcomed him inside. I saw that he was wearing dirty rags around his feet. I was taken aback and asked him about his discomfort.

"Of course, I'm in great pain," he replied, "but I'm heading home, and if that's the only price I have to pay to be free from the Germans, then that's cheap."

Inwardly, I agreed with him. I took some of the medication that the doctor had given me and dressed the man's bloody blistered feet as best I could. Not ever having cleaned open and infected wounds before, the procedure proved a trying experience. The man remained with us for about an hour. Then to my astonishment, he said that he was continuing his journey home. Through a bitter, biting wind, he vanished into the night. I believe we all understood, perfectly, why the man had left so suddenly.

We all tried to sleep as close to the fire as possible. The following morning, I discovered that a lapel of my coat was completely burned. Soon, everyone went their respective ways. I would head in the direction of Alvito, a village located in central Italy.

By evening, I arrived on the outskirts of a big valley, Val di Comino, fifteen miles in diameter. One could see clusters of houses at its edge, comprising little villages: Campoli, Atina, San Donato, Picinisco, Settefrati and Alvito.

Before entering Alvito, I made sure there were no Germans in sight. The narrow streets were barely paved, and the stone houses were constructed rather crudely. The area was quite hilly with very few places that were level. As I entered the village, its inhabitants looked at me suspiciously. A couple of women were carrying earthenware pots on their heads. A donkey transporting two barrels was urged on by a man switching a small twig. Everyone was staring at me. A woman standing at a doorway asked me if I was looking for someone. I told her that I was a refugee trying to get home and would she please tell me where I could spend the night.

"Well, there's the haunted house that is now empty; you could stay there." The woman explained that the previous couple died there under mysterious circumstances, pointing the house out to me. I asked her if I could have something to eat. She hesitated a moment before motioning me into her home. Her husband was in the process of eating, and he asked me to join him. They were having spaghetti.

"Food is becoming scarcer by the day," he said. "We get our white flour in Trasacco, in exchange for the corn we grow here."

Food was the most important aspect of their lives and played a major role in their daily activities. The man asked me where I was from. I told him Naples, and that the area was already occupied by the Allies. I felt that the man didn't believe me. He asked my name.

"Antonio Bruno."

"Ah, *bene.*"

I thanked the people for their hospitality and walked over to the "haunted" house. Ten steps led to a door with a crude handle. I entered a big room that had four windows. The place smelled moldy and musky. Some straw was piled in a corner. The fireplace held all kinds of debris: pieces of paper, empty cans and partly burned wood. The people here did all their cooking in the fireplace, using either earthen crocks or big kettles, which hung over the fire in order to boil water for polenta or spaghetti. I sat down on the straw with my back in the corner and looked myself over. My boots were in good condition. They were ankle high and offered me firm support on the uneven terrain. My pants had a few rips and needed repair. With the one lapel missing, my coat looked like a rag. My appearance would only prove worse for wear if I lost the other lapel. I looked down at my hands, turning them over slowly. They were the filthiest hands imaginable. I felt the thick stubble upon my face. I suddenly wanted to get out of the house and find a place to wash myself. But where? I got up and went over to a window and saw people standing in neighboring doors, staring in my direction. I gathered that the news of a stranger's arrival had traveled rather fast. I remained in the house when suddenly I became aware of an odd discomfort at the base of my spine. It was both painful and itchy at the same time. I touched the area and discovered a small swelling, choosing to ignore it.

Later, I walked to the edge of the village. It was frustrating to see the explosive flashes against the night sky and hear the sounds of artillery during the day. *Yes, the Allies would soon come over the mountains, and we'd all be free*, I entertained.

I was brought back to reality by the pain in my lower spine. That night, when I was huddled in a corner on the straw, I heard a knock on the door.

"Who's there?"

"Father Ponte."

I got up and let in a priest. He looked rather well-fed and bore a big smile. We shook hands, exchanging formalities. I felt the soft pudginess of his hand.

"My son, I heard of someone being here. Can I help you?"

"Well, Father, I'm of Jewish faith and would like for you to know that."

"Oh, but my son, the love of God is all-embracing for those that embrace Him, so don't you concern yourself with that. He looks out for his flock, and you are a part of that. You look rather underfed. Would you like me to bring some food tomorrow?"

"I would like that very much."

"Then I'll see you tomorrow around the same time."

He must have noticed my physical discomfort.

"Is there something wrong with your back?" he

asked.

I told him about the swelling, and he said that he'd have a look at it tomorrow.

Around the same time the following day, Father Ponte showed up with a big bowl of spaghetti and white beans.

"I'm sorry, Father, I can't even offer you a chair to sit."

"Oh, that's all right, Antonio. You go right ahead and eat, and while you do that, would you mind if I read something to you?"

"No, I wouldn't mind at all."

Father Ponte withdrew the New Testament and started reading a passage. I was so busy eating that I hardly listened to what he was saying. When I was finished eating, he wanted to look at the swelling at the base of my spine. After examining me, he suggested that I come to his home near the church because I would have to lie down on a table in order for him to do what had to be done.

That evening, I went to Father Ponte's house. He suggested that I first take a bath. Afterward, he told me to lie upon the table. He removed some surgical instruments from a bag.

"This may hurt a little bit, but you'll be all right after that."

I figured I'd experience a little pain, and that would be that. To my surprise, I felt such a jolt at the base of my spine, then passed out.

When I became conscious, I heard him say, "You behaved so bravely, Antonio. You didn't complain in the least. I'm proud of you. You may get up; it's all done. Can you walk?"

In spite of a little discomfort, I felt better and was able to walk fairly well.

"Come, I'll show you the church before you leave," he offered.

We walked out of the house and along a narrow street, coming upon a fairly spacious building for such a small community. We entered the church through a large front door. The interior held a rather musky odor. Father Ponte showed me all around. I was impressed by the colorful statues and beautiful ornamentation. It was a pleasant interlude.

"I'll see you tomorrow around the same time?"

"All right, Father," I replied.

The next day, he brought two small wooden boxes so that we could sit together. While I ate his food, he read to me from the Bible. He visited me daily, and I began to look forward to his company. After a week, he asked me a strange question.

"Do you see any light, Antonio?"

I did not understand what he meant.

"Don't worry about it; sometimes it takes time."

Daily, he continued to bring me spaghetti and beans, and when he had asked again if I see the light, I said to him, "You know, Father, I think I see the light in the far distance."

He seemed very pleased to hear me say it, so whenever he asked me that very question, I answered that the light seemed distant but was coming steadily closer. I had a sudden revelation that once I clearly saw the light, I would be out of my spaghetti and beans. Eventually, he became rather impatient and ultimately annoyed with me for not *distinctly* seeing the light, so I figured I may as well tell him that I finally saw the light. He was overjoyed.

"Perhaps you would like to come to one of our religious services."

"I believe I would, Father Ponte."

That night, the woman who had fed me on the day I arrived in Alvito came to see me, asking if I wanted to meet another refugee. I told her I would like to very much since I felt so lonely. I wouldn't even have minded talking to a cat. She asked me to follow her, leading me back to her home.

"This is Pierre," she said.

The man rose from a chair and extended his hand. I grabbed it with great warmth and enthusiasm. For a second, I was almost sorry I did because I thought that I was going to lose my hand. The pressure from his grip was powerful. My knees almost buckled. His strength was overwhelming. Standing before me was a narrow-shouldered, round-faced man in his late thirties. A broad smile uncovered two rows of black teeth. Thin lips, a big triangular and pointed nose, eyes of which one was grey and the other dark completed his features. He stood about five-foot-seven, wearing ankle-high boots and a pair of pants that ended three inches above his shoes.

"Pleased to meet you," he delivered in a huge bass voice that defied such a small frame. "Pierre Cavagna."

"Antonio Bruno," I replied, making sure that all of my fingers were still intact.

I told Pierre a bit about my background; likewise, he confided in an openly refreshing manner. He had spent a number of years in a prison in Northern Italy, being released when Italy capitulated. He had been sentenced by the Fascist government because he was very active in the anti-Fascist movement. Pierre was a graduate of the Sorbonne, a man who could discuss, in depth, a Shakespearean play or the merits of a Renoir. His knowledge of so many topics never ceased to astound me. Whenever he spoke on a particular subject, I was his best and, usually, only audience. He was born in Lyon, France, but for some reason never elaborated on his personal family life. Whenever I asked him about some mundane matter relating to his early life, he always managed to circumvent my inquiry, adroitly maneuvering around such questions whereby I'd find myself involved in some nonsensical discussion.

Pierre had an affinity for smoking black Italian cigars. Whenever he had one clenched between his black teeth, he appeared rather childlike, like a kid with a lollypop, which seemed to generate a greater calmness about him. The days that followed we spent together in the 'haunted' house.

One night, a very funny thing happened. Usually,

when we had to defecate, we would squat over a piece of paper and use an empty can to contain our urine. Then we would throw the feces and urine out back upon some rocks. I was asleep when suddenly awakened by Pierre's thunderous laughter and a terrible smell. I asked him what he found so funny in the middle of the night. He answered, gasping for breath, that he had just shit on the moon. After he calmed down, he explained that a hole in the roof permitted the moonlight to cast a spot on the floor, which he mistakenly thought to be a piece of paper. I joined him in his laughter, suggesting that next time he first feel for paper for fear his feces would burn a hole through the floor. We roared for a good half hour.

The following morning we awoke hungry, realizing that we were out of food. We went to the woman who had initially housed Pierre. She told us that her husband wasn't feeling well and that they were no longer in a position to give away any food. We went to several homes, but the families' responses were negative. Pierre suggested that I follow him to the square, and to my amazement, he posted himself right in the middle of it, spreading his arms widely.

"Ladies and gentlemen of this community," he called aloud. "You see before you two men who are desperately hungry. We have no food, our stomachs are empty, and we implore you to show your kindness and generosity."

People were gathering around us. They stood stoically, just staring at us.

"Looking at you, I cannot believe that you will permit two human beings to starve from hunger right before your eyes."

No response. They just kept staring.

Pierre's voice now boomed. "Oh, now I understand. I see why there is no response. It's because you want to be paid for food. Fine. There is no problem. Here is my wallet." He withdrew his wallet and, with a grand gesture, threw it upon the ground. "There, help yourself to what you feel is the proper payment for a plate of food. Go ahead. Don't be bashful."

I knew he didn't have a single lira in that wallet of his.

"All right, I get the message," he said very deliberately. "You want more than money. You want perhaps this item thrown in."

More people gathered around. Pierre removed his big brimmed hat and threw it down next to the wallet.

Next, he repeated the same with his jacket.

"How about that? That should pay for a small piece of corn bread."

No response. He started unbuttoning his shirt. This was going a bit too far, I thought.

"Here is my shirt," he continued. "That ought to satisfy you." He uncovered his chest and arms, exposing muscles that rippled with the slightest movement.

A woman came out of a house and walked over to Pierre, handing him a bunch of dried figs before she walked away.

"Finally, someone with a heart," Pierre stated. "Someone with feelings for the misery of her fellow human beings. God saw what this beautiful woman did, and He made note of it in His Golden Book." I knew that Pierre was a confirmed atheist. "The angels will accompany this woman for the rest of her life and provide safety and happiness for her."

Someone else came over with a small bag of onions.

"Good." Pierre spread his arms and lifted his face toward the sky, speaking heavenward. "Take notice of who is giving food to the needy and who is not, for at the time of final reckoning, judgment shall be passed, and the rewards will be just." He lowered his face and arms and looked around at the others. "And *your* punishments will be swift and without mercy."

A small boy came forward with a piece of bread. White bread. Jackpot!

Pierre continued his pleading, threatening and promising, but this was all that he could muster for the moment from these poor people. He got dressed, picked up his wallet and hat, and we went back to the 'haunted' house.

The two of us sat down and ate figs. Then he gave me all of the white bread and said, "Antonio, this is for you since you suffer so much from corn bread."

I insisted on sharing, but he wouldn't accept even the smallest piece.

Later, we decided to leave and head to the valley in search of food. We picked up our belongings and headed through the olive trees that grew on the outskirts of the valley, toward farmland. We followed a worn pathway and came to a farm that looked a bit more prosperous than the others. It was practically situated in the middle of Val di Comino. As we came closer, we could see a man of small stature working the field with a triangular spade. As we approached the house, he stopped working. We were about to knock on the door, when a woman in her mid-thirties appeared.

"We are refugees and are looking for some food. Could you spare something?"

She looked us up and down. "Oh, you must be *il Professore*," she said, facing Pierre. "And you," she added, addressing me, "the English spy."

Pierre and I exchanged looks. So that's what they chose to label us.

"If you want to help out around here, you may share the food we put on the table," the woman offered.

We agreed to help out, and for the next three weeks we worked and ate fairly well. The couple had one teenage boy who seldom spoke. He was very helpful to his parents.

The woman's name was Maria. She had a very dark complexion, high prominent cheek bones, large piercing eyes, a broad nose, and full lips that complemented her features. She was clothed in local fashion, wearing a long dark dress with a wide breast-supporting belt.

Maria was strongly built, and her hands were masculine looking. As I later learned, she could be both very tough and very generous. Maria's husband, Martino, was shorter, his head barely reaching her shoulder. Much like their son, Martino was a kind and quiet man who seemed happiest when he was working the field.

Fortunately, we didn't see any Germans around. The Allies were somewhere behind the mountains, north of Cassino. The war should soon be over. All the Allies had to do was cross one mountain chain and that would be the end of the Nazis, I believed.

Little did we know that it would take the Allies many more months of fighting to defeat the Third Reich. In the meantime, we had food and shelter. Pierre and I slept upstairs on boards that were supported by makeshift wooden legs. Atop the boards were bags filled with dried corn leaves that served as our mattress, along with two heavy brown blankets.

One day, I wasn't feeling up to par and remained in bed when Maria came up to bring me something to eat. The wall behind me served as my headboard on which was pinned a variety of photographs. Maria sat herself down on the edge of the bed and asked if I cared to know about the rest of her family. Of course, I said yes. She pointed to one of the photos above my head.

"This one is of my brother who lives in Alvito."

I couldn't see the picture because she was leaning

over me. Her bosom was about an inch from my nose. She was practically lying on top of me.

"And this young fellow is Michalooch. The rascal is always getting into some mischief, but I like him because he respects his parents. Can you see?" she asked.

I'd have to turn and stretch to see Michalooch. All I could see was her bosom.

From outside I heard Martino call her. She was annoyed and bent well across my body toward the window, putting her hand on my thigh for support.

"What do you want? I'm busy."

I heard Martino say something, and she replied, "All right, I'll be right down."

She withdrew from the window and looked at me with moist eyes that held an odd expression. She was breathing heavily. I didn't understand. She turned and left.

Why had she put her hand on my thigh? In flashback, I saw separate images of me, Paulette and Sergeant Piton in that barber chair in Barcelonnette . . . and understood perfectly.

As I was lying there in bed, from downstairs I heard excited voices belonging to Maria and Marco, the neighboring farmer. Maria came running back upstairs.

"Antonio, the Germans are moving into San Donato, Campoli and a few more towns; they started rounding up the men!"

Pierre came upstairs. "Let's get going, Antonio. Pack up and we'll head toward the high mountains."

Maria told us in detail of a place where there was a hidden cave that would shelter us from the elements. Within it, we could build a fire, and the smoke would dissipate among the boulders and not be visible to the outside. She gave us two bottles of wine. Pierre and I packed in no time, and off we went.

From a distance, we could hear Maria's Doberman barking. Pierre and I crossed the valley quickly, passing between San Donato and Picinisco, then steadily upward. We found the narrow path Maria had instructed us to follow. The ascent grew progressively cold. The terrain became exceedingly tougher to traverse. The sense of remoteness engulfed us. Pierre and I found it odd to see a religious statue surrounded by a fence. Maybe it was there so that passing farmers could spend a moment in prayer. We kept walking, and I was beginning to feel weak. Too often, I had asked Pierre to stop for a rest. He insisted we keep moving. There came a point when he removed my rucksack then swung it across and atop his own. I protested, but he told me to shut up. A short time later, we heard something.

"*Halten,*" someone ordered.

From behind a boulder, two soldiers in *Wehrmacht* uniforms appeared; rifles at the ready. Hanging from their necks by a silver chain was a prominent gorget displaying the name *Feldgendarmerie.*

"*Dokumente, du foule hunde.*"

Foul dogs? I steamed inside. *Why this tough talk?* They reminded me of Maria's Doberman.

Pierre spoke to the soldiers in Italian. "Please, you see here before you two tired refugees, lost in the wilderness. Could you please direct us? We are lost and we are looking for the protection of the Germans. Comrade!"

The two soldiers looked at one another, and one of them said in German, "What the hell is he saying?"

"No idea," responded the other.

I took out the green identification card stamped with the swastika that Captain Gribante had given me. The soldiers shouldered their rifles, examining the document.

Pierre looked at me while removing both rucksacks from his back.

"They don't understand Italian," I disclosed.

"Oh, those poor lovely little creatures," Pierre responded. "We have to be nice to them and help them do their job. After all, they are here to liberate all of us, and if they ask me for my documents, I'll have to show them." Pierre was grinning from ear to ear.

One gendarme returned my card while Pierre babbled on congenially. He put a hand inside a tattered coat pocket as if to hand over his documents, instantly withdrawing and leveling a handgun at one of the men's chest. In amazement, I watched Pierre deliberately shoot the soldier dead. The other German stood transfixed as Pierre put a bullet in the man's brain. Both cockroaches lay dead.

"So, you wanted my *dokumente*? You come on my soil and infect it with your presence. That is the document I have for you." Pierre turned to me. "Give me a hand, Antonio. Let's get rid of them."

Before we dragged then dumped the bodies over a precipice, we emptied their pockets. We helped ourselves to both rifles and ammunition.

I was still dazed by the event. Pierre knew that I was shaken.

"You see, Antonio, throughout history you will always find someone trying to subdue someone else by force. If we could only learn to do unto others as you would have them do unto you, there would truly be peace. We don't need a Bible to tell us this. It's just basic human common sense. But unfortunately, some people seem to think that they have the right to rule over others. Step back into history. What do you see? The Northern Italians fighting against those from the south; the Flemish against the Walloons—always people who are in proximity to one another. Have you ever heard of the Germans waging war against the Eskimos? Of course not. It's always against a neighbor. You can narrow that down to a family member against family member, internecine wrath or warfare. That's my philosophy in a nutshell. Show me your friendly intentions, and you become an extension of me. Try to burn me, and a great conflagration will be your doom. Ask me for documents with a gun, and I'll blast your ass off. I was born in France, but Italy is my home, and I don't like cockroaches in my kitchen."

"Are your parents still alive?" I asked. That question

was a mistake on my part. Pierre clammed up.

"Let's go to where we're going," he concluded quite stoically.

On that note, we continued onward.

CHAPTER NINE

Pierre and I finally came upon a fairly flat piece of real estate, about thirty feet in front of a vertical slit in the mountains.

"This must be it," I said.

As we approached the opening to the cave, out came a rather young man of about twenty years of age, pointing his pistol at us.

"Stop right where you are and raise your hands," he ordered.

We obliged.

"Who are you?" he demanded.

Two other men emerged from the cave. Pierre and I introduced ourselves and talked for a while, telling them what had happened within the last hour. The young man tucked the gun in his belt, stepped closer and grabbed our hands, planting kisses upon them. Pierre and I glanced at one another.

"You are welcome here," he stated sincerely, "and for the rest of your lives you have a friend in me. My name is Vincenzo Trombali, and these are two my brothers, Ferruccio and Leonardo. Let's go inside."

We followed the trio deep within the gut of the mountainside. A fire was burning. What little smoke rose from the fire was sucked up by a natural draft. We all sat down. As Maria had said earlier, any smoke or light from the fire would not be noticed from the outside.

"Vincenzo, why did you give us such an unusually warm welcome?" I asked.

With that, he stood up, turned and stepped away from us, then began sobbing uncontrollably. I was dumbfounded. Nobody said anything. Finally, he calmed down and rejoined us.

Composing himself, he said, "Forgive me for behaving this way. I'm a farmer, and we had a small place near Campoli. My father and mother also worked the farm. We had some pigs, chickens and some other farm animals. My sister, Loreto, worked just as hard as the rest of us. She was eighteen years old and engaged to a friend of mine who lived on the neighboring farm. Then one day the Germans came and took our pigs away. Then they came and took all of our sheep and goats. My parents pleaded to leave something for us, but they just laughed and helped themselves. A few days afterward, that's when it all happened. They came to take the chickens. My father resisted, and they shot him. I came out of the house with my mother when we heard the shot. There were three Germans. They started loading the chickens on a truck. We ran into the chicken coop where my father lay and died moments later. My mother and I ran back outside. She had a spade in her hand, and they shot and killed her, also. They shot me, too. I received a wound, here," he said, pointing to a scar that ran above his ear. "I became unconscious. When I came to, my mother was lying next to me. I ran into the kitchen." Vincenzo started sobbing again. "My sister was on the ground with a broomstick between her legs, which the bastards had pushed into her virgin body. She was naked. Before she died, she told me that they had raped her. The assassins wiped out my whole family over chickens. That's what they did. They killed and massacred what is dearest to me. My family. My life is completely broken."

We were all very quiet. Tears were rolling unashamedly down my face. When I lifted my eyes, I noticed that we were all in tears. It was very quiet. Pierre took out a bottle of wine which Maria had given to us and offered everyone. Nobody wanted any. He then proceeded to drink the whole bottle. I had the other bottle, and he asked me for it. Pierre emptied that one, too.

With one grey and one brown eye ablaze, Pierre finally rose unsteadily to his feet and walked to the mouth of the cave. I got up and followed him protectively. He stopped just outside the entrance and looked from left to right. I did not know what he was up to, but I felt very apprehensive. He walked twenty paces further, and the bright light of the full moon enveloped us. The stars were busy trying to outshine one another. Pierre looked ominous. He took a deep breath, and out of his thin sinewy body came a powerful bass voice. At the top of his lungs, he began to sing *La Marseillaise*, the French National Anthem.

"Allons enfant de la patrie," he sang, and I quickly joined him.

"Le jour de gloire est arrivé!"

Then Vincenzo, Ferruccio and Leonardo came out and joined in. They did not know the words but bellowed boldly while venting their rage along with us. The sound must have carried for miles and miles into the valley. I could visualize the German dogs listening and perhaps feeling a bit threatened.

"*Marchons! Marchons!*"

The sounds of revolt against the rapists. The murderers of innocent people. We had finished our singing and fell silent again. Pierre expanded his chest then slowly and deliberately bellowed into the night.

"German dogs, you came to rape and kill, but you will never leave Abruzzi alive. You will die there a horrible death."

He was perspiring. I took Pierre by the arm and turned him back toward the cave.

"Let's go inside," I coaxed.

We all went back inside. Not a word was said, and we decided to go to sleep.

It must have been a couple of hours later when Vincenzo shook me awake.

"I hear someone coming."

I got up, and the five of us stepped back behind a jagged stone formation ascending from the cavern floor, weapons at the ready. The footsteps came closer. To our surprise we saw two big haggard-looking men wearing strange uniforms.

"Hold it right there," Pierre commanded. "Who are

you?"

"We're Americans."

We came out from behind the rock formation, our weapons still trained on the pair. The men told us that they were shot down over Italy, captured and then sent to a prisoner of war camp. When the Italians capitulated, they were released and had been staying at different farms.

"We heard the French national anthem and thought that a French division was cutting through the German lines. We directed ourselves toward the singing, and here we are."

When they learned that it was only the five of us, the two looked at each other in disbelief. Both men stood over six feet tall, thin, in their mid-twenties. One had pronounced buckteeth.

"My name is John, and this is Warren."

We all shook hands, then sat around the dying embers when suddenly we heard the barking of big guns in the distance.

Please make it soon, Yankees, I thought as I fell back to sleep.

The following morning we shared what little food we

had and remained in the cave. Later, it was decided that someone had to go out and forage for food.

"Well, I don't mind going out and searching," I volunteered.

"I'll come with you," Pierre said.

"No, you'll stay here. I'll go scout around and see what I can find come nightfall."

Later that evening, I got ready to go out and hunt for food.

"Please be careful, Antonio," Pierre said.

The others echoed his warning, and I left.

It was so bright out that one could read a newspaper by moonlight. I carried my empty rucksack fashioned from a burlap bag. A knife, which I had with me from the days I belonged to the Belgian Scouts, along with my pistol, were both close at hand and felt comforting there in my pockets. I was walking for a time when I heard the sound of bleating. I followed the sound and came upon a corral of sheep. It appeared that no one was around, but I had to be sure. I waited awhile, then moved cautiously toward the edge of the corral. I climbed over and stepped within the enclosure. I did something then that for days would make me ill. I stealthily stepped forward, straddled a sheep, grabbed the animal under the chin and pulled back its head. In one swift motion, I slit the sheep's throat. It thrashed about as I grabbed its flailing legs. A moment later, I lifted and swung the wooly animal across my shoulders. As I was about to leave, a bantam lamb began to bleat, its cry sending shivers along my spine. The poor baby lamb attempted to follow me. I moved away rapidly, warm blood dripping down my neck and saturating my shoulders. I felt like a killer. I had slaughtered someone's mother. I was so guilt-ridden that I almost wanted to drop my burden and run away in shame, but I held tenaciously onto the animal's legs and kept on walking.

If the moon had not been so bright, I might have lost my way back to the cave. I was extremely fatigued and thought I might expire. When I reached our hideaway, the men congratulated me for my deed. Pierre swore that he would never let me out of his sight again. We were so hungry that we decided to roast the meat right away instead of waiting for the next day. We gutted and skinned the animal. The job left much to be desired, but we finally finished, throwing the whole animal upon the fire.

When we thought the meat was cooked, we all had

half-raw, half-charred mutton. But our bellies were full, enjoying the sensation that one can think much clearer on a full stomach than on an empty one. The seven of us chatted for a while. Before retiring, two stood guard at the mouth of the cave while five of us fell soundly off to sleep.

When I awoke that morning, I couldn't help notice the dried blood on my already filthy, dirty clothing. I decided, hopefully, to find a place to wash them. I shared my thoughts with the men, and they decided to do the same. We all went out in search of water. Eventually, we found a small stream. I got undressed and threw all my clothes in the brook then pounded them with a smooth rock. Within minutes, seven men were diligently washing their clothing.

I don't know how it started, but suddenly we were all throwing underwear at one another, standing stark naked and laughing like young children. Startled, I wound up with a dirty wet sock smack across my mouth. Seeing my reaction, my companions nearly choked with laughter, rolling and rollicking in the rather chilly water. Regaining composure, I rejoined them in their merriment.

Pierre and I had a change of dry clothing, but the others did not. Fortunately, the air temperature was warm, so after a few hours, they got dressed, even though their clothing was not completely dry. We were about to leave when we heard someone greet us.

"Hello there. I'm sorry I didn't come earlier. I would have joined you."

We saw a middle-aged man with bushy eyebrows carrying a case on his shoulder. It seemed to be heavy because when he put it down, it made a rather loud thumping sound.

"Tommaso, everyone calls me, and you may do the same."

We all introduced ourselves. As I approached the man, I asked him what was in the box.

"I don't know," he replied. "I was near San Donato, and the Germans were settling outside the village. I passed by an open truck that was unguarded and helped myself. Why don't we open it?"

"But we have to be very careful," I said.

"Why do we have to be careful?" Tommaso asked.

I realized he couldn't read. "Because it says **Ammunition** on the box."

We broke open the case, and it was filled with hand grenades. We looked at one another, and as we exchanged glances, we all started smiling. The eight of us, including Tommaso, instinctively knew what would soon transpire. My heart raced at the prospect.

Document #1

False identification provided by the partisans, identifying me as Antonio Bruno, an Italian national.

Document #2

A doctor, who was a member of the underground movement, provided me with another false document. He was subsequently caught by the gestapo and murdered.

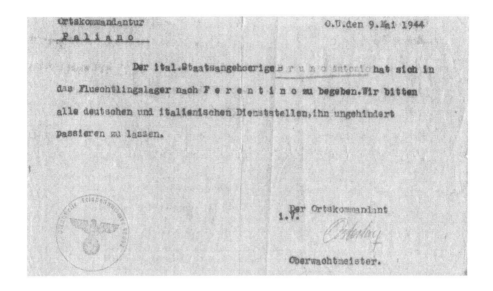

Document #3

Gustavo, an Italian prisoner I befriended earlier in time, served as an interpreter for the Germans. He facilitated the issuance of this pass, instructing all German and Italian authorities to allow me passage.

Document #4

Under my legitimate name, the Italian National Liberation
Committee issued me this pass one day after the
Germans withdrew from the area, heading northward.
This was liberation day from hell.

CHAPTER TEN

We spent the next three days scouting the area until we knew the topography fairly well. Vincenzo found that a road frequently used by German personnel was located below a spot where we could initiate an attack and get away quickly. We decided that we would stake out the place until we could see several trucks passing by. On the far side of the road, the mountain dropped off precipitously. John had shown us how to pull a grenade pin, instructing us to throw the small missile slowly so as not to sacrifice accuracy. We spent a couple of hours for the next several days waiting for a convoy while enjoying leftover mutton.

On the fourth day, I caught Tommaso's jaw drop as he peered past my shoulder. I turned to see a group of vehicles coming toward us in the distance. I broke out in a cold sweat. Pierre started grinning, showing his black teeth.

"Over here, pussy cats. That's right. Keep on

coming. Daddy's got nice hot candies for you. It's going to help your digestion. Keep on coming, krauts. Straight ahead. Free candy for all you lovely children." Pierre turned and faced us. "Okay, boys. Spread out, and remember what John told us. Don't rush. Focus on your target. Throw slowly and deliberately. Then back to the cave we go. This is for our families and friends and the liberation of enslaved people." Pierre appeared grim. "Antonio, you stay close to me."

We spread out at fifty-foot intervals, squatting down with a few grenades before us. The convoy approached in a steady column.

Vincenzo called out to us, "Please, allow me to have the first throw."

Pierre told him that on command, he should let the missile fly.

My mouth was dry, and I had to go to the bathroom badly. I could now discern the thick black crosses on the truck. The single row of vehicles was headed toward the front line. However, we would interrupt their destination, interceding with, as Pierre put it, candies for those pussy cats. *Yes.* Suddenly, I felt motivated, body and soul, forgetting about having to move my bowels. I became calm, very calm, and in full control of what I was about to do. I was totally focused, concentrating and calculating my premeditated action. I'd avenge my beloved ones . . . I'd avenge Vincenzo's sister, too.

"Now, Vincenzo! Now!" Pierre ordered.

I had my finger hooked into the grenade ring as I watched Vincenzo hurl his deadly candy. Bull's-eye. It hit the side of a truck. Then we all started peppering them. I envisioned *Dante's Inferno*. Our explosions ignited their munitions. Armageddon was in the making. German soldiers were jumping out of their trucks, running helter-skelter. Some found safety on the near side of the road. Others fell to their death down the steep side of the mountain. There were shouts and commands. Two trucks had toppled and disappeared down the deep decline.

We were out of grenades. The deadly business was over in a flash.

"Let's get out of here, now!" Pierre enjoined.

He grabbed me by the elbow, and we ran for our lives, ducking behind boulders as bullets spattered all around us, ricocheting off rocks that shielded us and the ground that gave us flight. Zigzagging, I followed Pierre's daffy dance as he led me by the sleeve at my elbow.

Finally, we reached the safety of the cave; our home

away from home. We were panting heavily, lying there at its mouth, utterly exhausted upon what felt like sacred ground. Pierre grabbed hold of my hand in his powerful grip, squeezing it . . . and I knew that we were friends forever.

"Don't worry, Antonio. I'll take care of you, my young friend."

He had, indeed.

When we caught our breath, I wondered what had happened to the others. Then we saw Tommaso with a bloody arm hanging limp at his side. In front of him walked a dazed German officer—his gun holster empty.

We ran over and quickly learned the bitter news. The other five men in our band had been killed. Tommaso thought it a good idea to capture this officer. Pierre helped Tommaso inside the cave, relieving him of the officer's pistol that had been pointed menacingly at the German's back. Pierre handed me the weapon and told me to guard the Nazi cur. I wrapped my fingers tenaciously around its grip, making sure the safety was off and a round seated in the chamber of the Mauser. I pointed the weapon at the officer's face. He turned grey.

"Take everything out of your pockets," I demanded in German.

A German cross and other iron garbage was hanging from his chest. On his collar was the SS insignia. As he emptied his pockets, we stared at each other.

Wouldn't it be something, I thought, if he retrieved a hidden weapon like in the western movies, then I could blast him away without compunction. Oh, how I hated his face and his meaningless medals.

"Step back," I said.

His face changed completely. I noted a breast pocket that he hadn't opened.

"Open up that pocket and take everything out. This is the last time I'm going to tell you."

He reluctantly opened a breast pocket and retrieved two letters and a small pouch.

"Sit down on the ground with your back to me."

He promptly followed my command.

Pierre walked over to me. "Tommaso fainted and has lost an awful lot of blood. I applied a tourniquet," he said rather sadly. Pierre stared down at the keys, wallet and other items that the German officer had removed from his pockets. Pierre picked up the pouch and one of the letters.

I opened the other letter and translated aloud:

Dear Fritz,

Keep on sending the gold rings. There is a good market for them. When you come home on leave, you will be surprised how the cache has filled since you were here last.

I paused and saw Pierre's eyes glaze over and appear trance-like. His face turned to stone. I stopped reading and opened the pouch, finding it fairly full of wedding bands. One bore the inscription, *Love forever, 1934.*

"Ask him, Antonio, if he had ever prayed in his miserable little life."

I translated, and Fritz answered in the negative. He was perspiring heavily.

"Tell him he has five minutes left to live. Then he is going to die."

Pierre took the Mauser from me. I related my friend's message.

The officer spoke shakily. "Look, they were dead; they didn't have any use for them anyway. If I didn't take them, someone else would have."

"Did you steal their chickens?" I asked.

He looked at me strangely.

"You know I'm a Jew," I said.

"Oh, are you? This is wonderful because my best friends are Jewish. I even lived on a street where there were Jewish people. I am truly very fond of them."

"Them? Is that so? The truth of the matter is that you belong in a cattle car to be gassed with the rest of *your* kind. You are a pig, a swine."

I translated our dialogue for Pierre.

"Tell him to stand up. He's got two minutes," Pierre stated flatly.

I informed the Nazi swine of the countdown.

"I am an officer of the Third Reich; you'd better surrender," he said haughtily as he rose to his feet.

"One minute," Pierre said solemnly.

I translated anew.

"Please, please. I didn't mean it." The officer fell to his knees. "I beg for mercy. Please let me live. I'll return the rings, and I won't take them anymore, I promise. I swear. I'll—"

The Mauser sounded, and Fritz clutched his chest,

holding on to one of his medals before keeling over on his side.

We dragged him several yards to the edge of a cliff and sent him sailing through the air, watching and listening to the thudding sounds as he tumbled steadily downward along the stony slope. Suddenly, the body stopped, and a small cloud of dust arose. Dust and the elements would be his shroud. We stood there for a moment in silence before heading back to the cave to attend to Tommaso.

To our sorrow, the poor fellow lay dead. All I could think about was the waste of human life. So much destruction. *Please make this nightmare stop*, I pleaded to God.

We put Tommaso to rest by burying him under a pile of rocks. It seemed to take forever. When we finished shortly before nightfall, the two of us were completely spent. Retiring to the cave, we fell fast asleep.

The following morning we decided to leave the cave and try to obtain some food from farmers. I walked over to the pile of rocks and put my hand upon it. Pierre did the same.

"May you have peace in heaven, Tommaso," I said.

"Oh, come on, Antonio, there is no such thing as heaven. For Tommaso the war is over. Life is for the living. Let's go, my friend."

Pierre made me think hard and long about such things as heaven and hell and life and death. I'm alive, but tomorrow I may not be so lucky. A bullet could snuff out my life as quickly as extinguishing a candle flame. I had witnessed this all too frequently.

The Allies will never be able to break through the German lines, I reflected rather pessimistically. *The Allies will be held at Cassino for the next forty years! Months have already gone by, and if the Americans, with their unerring weapons, have not been able to dislodge the Germans, nobody ever will*, I complained inwardly. *Unless . . . .* I stopped internalizing and spoke to Pierre.

"Pierre. How about we head for the front lines immediately and thus shorten our suffering? I think it's worth a try."

"Good idea, Antonio, but I would suggest waiting another few weeks. If nothing happens, then we'll make an attempt."

CHAPTER ELEVEN

For the next several weeks, we roamed the area. To my great dismay, the local farmers started calling me, "The English spy with the radio transmitter." Pierre was given the moniker, "*Il Professore.*" Every time I tried to persuade the people that I was not a spy, they would say, "You see my mouth? *Mi bocca?* It's never going to reveal the secret that's entrusted to me, as the Holy Madonna is my witness."

"But I'm not a spy," I insisted.

"*Aspètto.* My mouth is like a grave; and in it is buried a secret from this moment on until I'm facing my Maker."

"But I'm not—"

An outstretched palm faced my nose. "Ah, by the way, what's the news on your secret radio?"

As I was about to protest, an idea struck me. "All right, but this mustn't go any further."

The sign of the cross was formed upon the farmer's forehead in reply.

"There is a major division of Allied tanks strategizing a pincers movement, concentrating the maneuver around Cassino. But I don't know the exact date. That's all I can tell you for now."

I saw the glimmer of hope light in the farmer's eyes.

"*Bene, bene*! My wife will prepare spaghetti with beans tonight, and my family and I will honor the table with both *il Professore* and you, the English spy!" he swore proudly.

"Shh!" I warned the man, bringing a finger to my lips to seal the secret.

"*Scusi.* I'm so sorry," the farmer apologized profusely. "I didn't mean to speak so loudly."

So it was that I always had something of a surreptitious nature to say to the local farmers; and although my news wasn't always true, it was what became expected of Pierre and me. It gave the families hope and provided Pierre and me with full bellies. We all benefited.

One morning Pierre suggested that we go back to Alvito to see Martino and Maria. As we were usually of one mind, we implemented plans expeditiously. So off we went in the direction of Alvito, making sure to avoid the Germans, giving hope to the farmers and eating spaghetti or polenta along the way. We pretty well knew where the Germans were stationed for miles around: positioned behind rocky ledges, or concealed under camouflage nets that were practically invisible from the air. It was a Sunday when we arrived on the outskirts of Alvito, where we were greeted by an older man.

"Ah, the English spy and his companion *il Professore*. Come to my house and tell me the latest news."

We followed and entered his humble home.

"The Americans have just brought over thousands of mules," I fabricated. "The soldiers are planning a nocturnal penetration toward the German lines. As you know, these sure-footed animals are better suited than horses. Upon the mules' backs they'll be carrying small but special canons that have tremendous range and accuracy." I paused for the full effect. "Please don't force me to say anything further. I'm sure you understand my position."

"Bravo, Antonio," the man replied quite happily. "You are a great spy and know that my mouth is sealed."

A neighbor came by and entered the man's home. "Hello, *Professore* and Antonio," he greeted like he had known us all of our lives. "I've just heard from a reliable source, I cannot tell you who, that the American are going to soon advance behind Cassino with a half million tanks, encircling the Germans. This will happen in five days. I promised my friend Roberto not to tell a soul. Let's share some wine I brought in early celebration."

With that announcement, the neighbor produced what he said was a heavy-bodied, powerful local wine. I usually abstained because I didn't care for it that much. Also, because Pierre had a tendency to get intoxicated, and I was the one who wound up taking care of him.

The three were drinking for about an hour when I suggested to Pierre that we head toward Val di Comino. Pierre wasn't too steady on his feet, so I supported him under an arm while we walked along uneven streets.

Sometime later, I saw two German soldiers coming out of a house, and they looked at us very suspiciously. I turned my eyes away from them and casually walked a staggering Pierre around a corner. I could hear the Germans picking up their pace. And so did Pierre and I. We turned another corner, and I heard them following us.

I saw Father Ponte's church door ajar. "Pierre,

quickly, into the church." I dragged Pierre through the door. As we moved forward, I took Pierre's and my rucksack and tossed them over a partition. To my surprise, I saw Maria, her daughter, Seraphina, and others on their knees. I recognized most of the other faces. I went to my knees alongside Maria, but Pierre just stood there swaying, still wearing his large brimmed hat.

"Pierre, on your knees, please."

"I don't kneel for statues or people."

"Please, Pierre, take off your hat and kneel."

Behind us someone said, "*Professore*, you are standing between me and God."

Pierre staggered. "When I see Him, I'll tell Him where you are."

"Please, Pierre, for the country of your childhood. For Vincenzo, Ferruccio, Leonardo, John, Warren and Tommaso," I rattled off. "For Vincenzo's sister, mother and father."

Pierre's knees bent, and his hat came off as he kneeled. Father Ponte turned from the altar and saw me. His eyes glistened in recognition, and a smile graced his face. He continued Mass. Maria put her hand on my head and pushed me down, reaching across and doing the same to Pierre. I was enveloped by a scarf and a part of Maria's skirt. I heard the Germans' boots stop outside the church, then resume their hurried steps. Again, I got that sensation of having to go to the bathroom real bad.

We stayed until Mass was almost over. Then Father Ponte made the sign of the cross, specifically toward me, turned, and with widespread arms, looked upward toward an immense crucifix. *If it'll help, Father Ponte, I'll accept anything*, I thought. The service was over, and the whole congregation went their separate ways. I picked up our bags and followed Maria and Seraphina at a distance so as not to endanger them. Down into the valley we went, following the two women.

We passed a neighbor's farm, and I could hear Maria's Doberman barking in the distance. I felt a chill from its sound. When we were well into the valley, Pierre and I caught up with Maria and Seraphina.

"The Germans are all over," Maria warned, looking at me with obvious concern. "We have to be so careful."

Pierre nudged me with his elbow. "She likes you, you lucky fellow," he said to me in French.

I was very embarrassed.

We finally arrived at the farm. It felt like home. The

smell of the fireplace. The crude furniture. It all started to grow on me. *Where are my mother and father?* I wondered. *What has happened to them?*

We all sat down. Maria served soup into which we dunked some white bread.

"You know," she said, "some time ago, we heard the French troops singing the *Marsaillaise* in the mountains. It happened when three German soldiers stopped here for some water. When they heard the singing, you should have seen how quickly they ran out and back to their posts. I guess, however, the French couldn't penetrate the lines. I heard earlier that the Americans are bringing in many mules to carry a lot of ammunition over the mountains for their next attack. Let's hope the Santa Maria will watch over the Allies."

Pierre and I exchanged looks. Martino entered and gave us a hearty welcome. Maria put up some water for Pierre and me to bathe. We felt so much better after hot soup and a warm bath.

Prior to that latter luxury, I had experienced terrible itching, discovering that I had lice. No matter what I did, it was impossible to get rid of them. Pierre was afflicted by the same pest.

After Pierre and I helped out with chores around

the farm, we went upstairs and fell into a deep sleep. We slept soundly through the evening.

The next morning I rekindled the fire by first stoking still hot cinders covered with ashes. A few dried twigs and a breath through a long, tapered metal pipe was all that was needed for the flames to glow anew. Pierre and I had a light breakfast before going to work in the field next to Martino.

For lunch, Maria came to us with corn bread.

"I love to feed you, Antonio," she said rather forwardly.

I felt embarrassed.

She looked at me coquettishly, and I understood her intent. If Martino hadn't been in the picture, the situation might have been different. But I wasn't going to let anything happen because the man had welcomed me into his home. I would not betray his trust and hospitality. I made believe that I didn't understand Maria's meaning, but Pierre's manner and silly behavior didn't help matters: smiling, raising his eyebrows and winking at me openly from beneath his big hat, clenching a thin crooked black cigar between two rows of black teeth—a cigar that Martino had given him.

Martino came over to us and said that he needed a rake. "The one I had broke yesterday," he explained. "I'll go over to my neighbor, Sarno, and borrow his until I fix mine."

"I'll do that for you," I offered.

Martino thanked me, and I headed off to Sarno's farm, which was situated about three quarters of a mile from us.

Martino, I had discovered, wasn't a bright man, but he would give the shirt off his back to help a person in need. I grew very fond of him. How I wished I had a father like him, endowed with basic goodness and kindness.

Sarno's place looked like the rest of the farms in the area. The home was crudely built with stones, which were abundant. Sarno had two cows, a donkey, chickens and lots of sheep. He owned lots of land. The man had spent thirty years in the United States, saved most of his money and bought the property from the owner to whom he used to pay rent.

Sarno welcomed me with a warm greeting. "Come and join us, Antonio. Any news on the secret radio?"

"I received a message recently from high sources that Czech and Bulgarian mountain climbers are planning a nocturnal assault with flame throwers, but the exact date I do not know. However, it's going to be soon. That much I know for sure."

Sarno's wife, Magdalena, a plump jolly-looking woman, their daughter, Amanda, a plain-looking woman of about thirty, and their son, Giuseppe, all stopped chewing as I spoke. When I finished my fictional account, the family simultaneously resumed their munching. We sat in silence when suddenly I felt Amanda's knee exerting pressure against mine. I withdrew it slightly, but she persisted. I had flashbacks to Paulette's barber chair and Maria's advances. Somewhat aroused, I imagined the table rising before me.

"What's the matter?" Sarno asked.

"Oh, nothing. Just something that happened some time ago."

I stayed until dark, borrowed Sarno's rake and said good-night to everyone. As I was leaving, the man came up to me.

"May you go with the protection of God," Sarno stated solemnly.

I thanked him and disappeared into the darkness. As I passed the barn, I heard Amanda call out to me in a hushed voice. It was so dark I couldn't see her.

"Over here, Antonio."

I stepped back to the barn, pausing by the door.

"Would you like to stay with me for a while?"

I felt my knees buckle. I was highly aroused. *This is it, Sam,* I knew . . . resounding cymbals, blaring trumpets, fireworks! *Finally . . . no more fantasizing. This is the real thing, fella. Put the rake against the wall and go man. Don't be weak and stupid. No moralizing, just submit to the call of nature.*

Amanda took me by the wrist and drew me into the black cavity of the barn. There was a passionate embrace. She pushed me solidly against what I thought was the side of a stall, but it moved, turning out to be the hind quarter of a cow. I stepped away from the animal. *What the hell do I do now?*

She started petting me, and I followed suit. I was out of my mind with lust. I felt something at my shoulder. *Maybe if I held on to it and put my leg over . . . no, that's no good.* Her skirt was long and voluminous. I felt a bale of hay. *Maybe she ought to sit on the bale, and then I'll sit on her lap. No. That's no good.* I lost my balance and hung on to whatever it was that I felt at my shoulder. The confounded thing came off the wall and fell. *Somebody help me.*

Breathing heavily, Amanda whispered, "Get down on the ground; lie down."

Of course, how stupid of me. I stretched out upon my back. The ground felt so good, so soft. *Sam, very soon you'll be a real man.*

"Amanda, where are you?" Sarno called out in the night.

"I'm in here, Father. I'll be just a moment." Then Amanda whispered to me, "Next time, Antonio. I've got to go now."

She left me lying there on the ground. As I started to get up, I felt something queer at the back of my neck. I touched my nape. To my great dismay, I realized that I had been lying in the droppings of the cow. It was destined I would not become a man tonight—maybe never! The forces of nature were against me. I would either die from a German bullet or shriveled testicles.

My groin hurt as I headed back to Martino's farm. I was filthy, covered with dung. I had to invent a story to explain my appearance.

As I walked into the kitchen, I found Martino,

Maria, Claudio, Seraphina and Pierre seated around the table. They all looked up at me oddly.

"What's that smell, Antonio?" Pierre questioned.

"Oh that. It was so dark in Sarno's barn I couldn't see where I was going. I tripped on something and almost fell on the rake. Yes, you see, the rake was supposed to be near the door, and I finally found it." That sounded credible. I waited for their reactions.

"Turn around, Antonio," Pierre said.

By now the cow dung had partially dried on my back, neck and shoulders. I turned around, and then they all burst out laughing.

"Stinky Antonio!" Maria exclaimed between gasping breaths of laughter.

"No, it's Antonio Shit Boy," cried Pierre with laughing eyes.

I must have been some sight standing there with the rake in my hand and manure all over my back. The kids were laughing, too. I thought I might as well join their merriment.

"How dare you speak to me in such a tone? I am the king of the Val di Comino, and this is my royal scepter." I lifted high the rake.

They were screaming with hilarity.

"And what you smell, you lowly mortals, is Royal Nectar to attract the queen." I couldn't continue, for I was caught up in their mirth.

My audience was speaking and laughing hysterically. Quite loudly. The jumble of words was incoherent. Suddenly, their laughter stopped abruptly as if an invisible sword had severed everyone's vocal cords. Our fit of laughter was upstaged by the ferocious barking of the family's Doberman. Five sets of eyes focused and fixed on something behind me.

I turned to find two *Feldgendarmen* standing in the doorway. My first impulse was to reach for my weapon, but I kept my cool. We all stood still as stone, staring at one another.

One of the soldiers smiled and spoke in German. "These Italians are a real stinking lot, but this one smells especially foul—I mean like cow shit. Let's get out of this hole." The pair turned and left.

I went directly to the door, and when I was sure they were out of earshot, I translated what the Nazi dog had said. Our moment of merriment ended as quickly as it had begun.

With Maria's and Martino's permission, I washed up before Pierre and I headed upstairs. A few minutes later, Maria came up and collected my clothing to wash. A time later, we all went to bed.

In the middle of the night, Pierre poked me.

"Wake up, Antonio. I think it's time we cross the front lines as you had suggested earlier . . . unless you changed your mind. I have to join the Allies in order to fight the enemy more effectively."

"Of course I'll come. It's what I set my mind to do from the very beginning. You know that."

I didn't sleep the rest of the night. The next morning we told Martino and Maria of our intentions. It was a very emotional scene. Maria, Martino and Seraphina broke down and unashamedly wept. They packed some dried sausages, a loaf of bread, dried figs and a bottle of wine. I assured them that we'd return one day, and if for some reason we couldn't, we'd write. Pierre and I would never forget them. How could we?

"Yes, we will be very careful," I promised Maria.

We said our good-byes and left, listening to the growling sounds and incessant barking of the family's Doberman.

CHAPTER TWELVE

Pierre and I headed straight for the front lines, following in the direction from where we saw flashes of light at night and heard the artillery throughout the day. We had to pass Picinisco again, which lay in our path. We marched silently and steadily along.

After a spell, Pierre broke the silence. "If not today, my friend, then probably by tomorrow we'll make it across to the Allies and be able to breathe unpolluted air."

Pierre turned quiet again.

"Pierre, if we do make it across, I want to have a good meal . . . no, I mean an excellent meal, and then I want to experience what it's like to be with a woman."

Pierre grinned, displaying his black teeth. "The meal I can promise you. The woman you'll have to fetch yourself."

We could faintly hear Maria's Doberman barking in the distance. A short time later, the barking stopped. I thought nothing of it. Pierre, however, sensed something amiss. He turned and paused. I saw a strange look cover Pierre's face.

"Take out your pistol, Antonio, and put your bag down, quickly." I followed his orders.

"Do as I do." He went down on one knee and held his right wrist with his left hand, holding his weapon outward. In the distance, I saw the black Doberman swallowing the distance between him and us. It started barking again—ferociously—dragging a length of chain. I felt the hair at the back of my neck rise.

"Shoot when I shoot. Slowly. Don't pull, but *squeeze* the trigger." Pierre spoke in a subdued tone. "Slow and easy."

The dog's mouth and breast were covered with white slaver. I squeezed the trigger a nanosecond after Pierre shot. The Doberman dropped instantly and lay dead before us.

What made this animal so enraged? I wondered. Just like the Nazis, full of hate and fury. As with the Nazis, we never did anything to harm the beast.

"We better get out of here because the Jerries may want to investigate those shots. But first things first."

Pierre stepped over to the dead dog, lying there with its teeth fixed in a snarling pose.

"Give me your knife, Antonio."

I gave it to him, and without saying another word, he dressed and butchered the dog. "Tonight we'll have canine stew," he said.

I didn't mind, for I had alleged rabbit stew prepared from cats. Although I wouldn't dream of eating cat or dog today, I'm reminded of the fact that when one is hungry, one will eat anything. I remember a scene from *The Gold Rush*, starring Charlie Chaplin, in which he ate a shoe.

Pierre and I carried quartered sections of Doberman. We had a standard way of cooking stew that was a specialty. The head chef of Le Cordon Bleu could take a lesson from us.

We made a fire, took a pot which we carried along for our *gourmet* meals, filled the pot with water, submerged the raw meat, and after boiling the water for a while, *Viola!* Stew Bourguignon al la Pierre/Antonio. One thing was for certain. After having eaten, we could, once again, think clearly.

Pierre and I passed through Picinisco, having walked along lovely rows of olive trees. Up ahead was a spot where the Germans had set up a storage depot, covered with camouflage netting. Pierre and I knew several of these locations. If only the Allies knew the information that we possessed.

The two of us skirted that mountainous area by a considerable margin, climbing higher and higher along narrow paths. I spied and pointed out the same religious statue I had seen that moonlit evening when I left the cave and went hunting for food. Passing close to the fence that encircled the figure was any number of coins lying on the ground near the base of the statue. Farmers passing by would throw the Italian lira as a matter of custom, and the local priests would later retrieve them.

Pierre climbed over the small fence and started picking up some coins.

"What are you doing, Pierre?" I chastised. "That is not your money; leave it there."

"That's where you are wrong, my friend. If I don't pick it up, the local priests will. Look at me, Antonio. Am *I* not in need of help? Look at yourself. Are you not in need of assistance and support? Just look at the two of us. All of the priests I've met have big bellies in spite of their vows of living a modest life. I think they're having a ball. Yes, indeed. I think that religion is working fairly well for them, and I think that now's the time for us to receive our share."

When Pierre had gathered all the coins, he turned to the statue, took off his hat, bowed and said, "I appreciate what you have done for us, and if I've disturbed you in any way, I profoundly apologize, Madonna." He put on his hat and climbed back over the fence.

We always made it a point to make a fire before dark so as not to expose our whereabouts. Since we had no water to cook Doberman stew, we roasted the meat.

I remember having gone squirrel hunting with a friend in Barcelonnette. The boy's name was Rissi, and he was deadly with a slingshot. Before the hunt, I watched him pick up a stone, put it in the sling and pull back. The stone made a lazy arch through the air and, from one hundred feet away, smashed with tremendous force against an old rusty padlock that shattered under impact. With unerring accuracy, he would kill squirrels. To my astonishment, squirrel meat tasted very good. Not at first, but one learns to develop a taste. Now, we were eating dog. Doberman, no less. It's strange how in the western world we look with contempt at other cultures for eating certain animals. We condemn various Third World countries for eating animals that we keep as pets, sharing our shelter and giving them endearing names. Yet we condone our slaughterhouses, which are, the truth be known, not always operated under compassionate conditions. Ah, but when hunger strikes our being, one changes one's philosophy very quickly. Better to eat dog than a shoe; right Charlie?

We had an uneventful, restful evening before getting an early morning start.

"We're going to cross Monte Meta tonight," Pierre said. "We'll keep off trails and paths today as best we can. Then tonight, we'll make an attempt to cross the front lines. If we're lucky, we'll be free by tomorrow. God willing."

I stared rather doubtfully at Pierre, for the mountainous terrain was very steep and rugged. Progress was extremely slow. It was getting quite cold. We proceeded with great caution, steadily and steeply upward. Patches of snow were visible along the peaks.

Finally, the terrain started leveling off before descending steeply. Suddenly, we were vertically challenged, our bodies leaning back out of the perpendicular to keep from sliding and falling forward. Soon, we adapted and found our footing. A short time later, we were upon solid ground.

It grew so quiet that I became aware of Pierre's breathing, mixed with my own. Eventually, we reached a point near dense shrubs. Suddenly, we could see for miles, deep down into a valley that had vehicles running along a road—vehicles that were most definitely *not* German. My heart jumped. *Soon Sam, you'll be free. You'll have a royal meal followed by delicious desserts: chocolates and fruits and all kinds of goodies. You'll play morra with Pierre; but instead of wine for the prize, it's going to be champagne accompanied by a delicious woman. My woman, for I'm going to be the winner!*

My reverie was interrupted by approaching footsteps. Pierre and I crouched quickly into the brush to break our outlines and blend with our surroundings. We didn't move a muscle. The footsteps came closer. We heard a dog bark, then from behind a boulder a German soldier appeared.

"Hide your gun, quickly," Pierre ordered.

I withdrew my weapon and lodged it within the branches of brush. Pierre did the same. The dog was aware of our presence. It was raising hell. The soldier raised his automatic weapon, pointing it in our direction. He saw us.

"Aufstehen! Los!"

Pierre and I stood and stepped out from the brush with our hands raised.

The soldier motioned for us to walk in front of him, commanding the dog to be quiet. The shepherd immediately obeyed.

I felt defeated. I thought it best if he simply pulled the trigger now, since I was never going to get out of this elevated hell alive. We walked a distance, down to a base camp and were directed toward a large wooden structure that stood in the center. A number of German military personnel eyed us when we approached the area. Our captor motioned us to step inside the framework. We entered a room with makeshift furniture standing against the wall. A big table sat in the middle of the room.

"I brought you more customers, Lieutenant," the German soldier stated with a big smile. "They were trying to cross the lines like the rest of them."

"Search them," replied the officer to his subordinate.

A sudden chill took hold of me as another German soldier ran his hands along my body, miraculously passing over the knife in its sheath at the small of my back. The pistol they certainly would have found hadn't Pierre told me to discard it. Had we shot the soldier and the shepherd back by the brush where Pierre and I were hiding, the entire camp would have been upon us within minutes.

"Search their bags," ordered the lieutenant.

There was nothing suspicious for them to find. The searcher bore an expression of disgust after searching through our rags.

"Nothing, Lieutenant."

"All right. Take them upstairs with the other garbage."

I almost complied with his command but caught myself. Had I taken a step toward the stairs, I would have revealed that I understood German. Someone poked us in the back and led us to a wooden staircase.

As Pierre and I climbed the stairs to the rafters, we entered a shallow, dim space directly beneath the roof. I saw approximately thirty men sitting or stretched out. We were heartily welcomed by the group and quickly learned that most of them had the same idea in mind: to get across the lines and fight the enemy. Pierre and I squatted down and peered through a slit in the rough-hewed floorboards. We could see the Germans milling about. I could hear what they were saying without any difficulty. Nobody seemed to know what was in store for us.

Pierre struck up a conversation with an elderly gentleman named Gustavo. The man had been some sort of instructor at a university. He and Pierre discussed ancient Greece civilization before veering off to Goethe. The discussion continued, delving into the sexual implications of Mephistopheles in Gounod's *Faust*. Next, they talked about Bach's chord structure. I sat in awe of these two men, and while I did not understand a fraction of what they were saying, I was deeply impressed by their knowledge.

While the two were conversing, I retrieved a few dried figs. Gustavo saw me eating and immediately terminated the discussion. He excused himself, saying that he was tired and wanted to sleep. He lay in a fetal position, and I saw the look of hunger in his eyes, a look I knew, unfortunately, all too well. I nudged Gustavo and pressed three figs into his palm. He took them, then held my hand in silent gratitude.

Late that night I was kept awake by snoring, flatulence and nightmarish moaning. From downstairs I could hear subdued voices.

"What will we do with all those people upstairs, *Herr Oberleutnant?*"

"We'll take them to Sora and probably finish them off there."

There was no elaboration as to how our captors were going to accomplish this, but being aware of what they intended to do would give Pierre and me an edge. I would have liked to reveal my knowledge to everybody, but that would eliminate any chance for the two of us to attempt an escape.

I woke Pierre up and whispered what I had just learned.

"Antonio, nobody here must know what you have just found out if we are to have the slightest chance of escaping," he stated emphatically.

We were of like minds, confronted by a deadly dilemma.

It was well into the night before I finally fell asleep . . . unconsciousness eventually giving way to conscience.

After what seemed like a brief moment of rest, we were all rudely awakened by the barks of a German soldier.

"Up! Get up, you lazy bastards! Up!" he ordered in German, though everyone got the gist.

Like cattle, we were herded and driven downstairs and outside into the cold air, squinting in the bright light of day. I saw another thirty men, obviously captured sometime earlier. I wondered where they had spent the night.

Gustavo approached an officer, and in impeccable German, he said, "Officer, I speak fluent Italian and German. Could I be of any use to you? I was an instructor at a university."

The officer was genuinely surprised. "I think we can find something for you to do. Follow me."

Gustavo walked off with the officer.

Moments later, someone gave each of us a piece of black bread, and I immediately thought about the truck in Rome.

"Everyone line up in a single file, please," Gustavo ordered us in Italian, standing alongside the officer. Then the German officer told Gustavo to rejoin the rest of us. Gustavo stood in front of me.

It had rained heavily the night before, and there

were large pools of standing water surrounding the area, several of which were shallow puddles covered with thin films of ice. I felt dirty and cold. We were all shivering. I looked around and saw men of all ages. Some bore a dignity about them, a deportment from which their dirty clothes would not detract. Others looked and behaved like their clothing implied: filthy wretches.

I recalled several individuals I knew back home who wore very expensive clothes. However, their finery could not conceal the vulgarity of their nature the minute they opened their mouths.

We all stood there for a time, still quivering from the cold when I heard a German officer mention that we were being transported to Sora. I knew that come what may, we mustn't ever reach Sora. I whispered to Pierre what I overheard. Composed, he pulled the brim of his hat down tightly. Pierre always appeared quite comical that way, but I knew that a deadly business was brewing in his mind. I trusted that man with my life.

We were standing face to face. I could read the urgency in his eyes; the light one and the dark one.

"When I say run, we run," Pierre said softly.

That's all he said, and I felt that we would somehow be all right. It's what I desperately needed to believe.

Gustavo stood directly in front of me; Pierre behind me. Two assigned soldiers shouldering a rifle covered the front and rear of the line. We were ordered to move ahead.

If the guard with the dog hadn't spotted us earlier, Pierre and I could have crossed the line and been in friendly territory by now, or maybe we'd have wound up dead. Shot in the back or blown up by other Germans, or maybe . . . . I began to see the futility of my suppositions, assuming this and that. I felt bitter and frustrated. The fact is that Pierre and I were *here*, and we'd have to tackle this problem the best way we could. I started to think positive, pleased about my mountain boots, noting what some of these poor prisoners had to endure, not having the proper foot gear. Some had just rags around their feet, held together with string.

We all marched forward in single file. There was a slow descent. I noticed Gustavo having difficulty walking. I reached out and held him under an arm.

He raised his eyes to mine, and his lined face broke into a big smile. "Thank you so much." After awhile, he disengaged himself from me. "I'll be all right now," he said. Everything was still wet when we reached the lower area of the mountain. Large pools of water were everywhere. It started clouding up again. About a half an hour later, God must have opened the zipper that contained all the rain water of Europe. It came down in such volume that we were drenched to the bones in seconds. Then as suddenly as it had started, the downpour abruptly stopped, and the warmth of the benevolent sun shone upon us. We came to the edge of Val di Comino and the terrain became very familiar.

Nonchalantly, Pierre edged his way between Gustavo and me. The mountain water had collected swiftly, connecting puddles and pools that now ran along great expanses, manifesting themselves most magically into narrow shallow streams. Pierre was deliberately walking at a snail's pace, seemingly to avoid the cursory flow of water at his feet. However, he was taking an inordinate amount of time. I didn't understand what Pierre was doing at first when suddenly it became abundantly clear what he was up to. The two of us were situated in the middle of the file, and by lagging behind, Pierre had extended the line, creating a blind stretch at the bend up ahead along otherwise open terrain. The German soldier at the rear of the column came up to us and motioned that we catch up with the men in front. Pierre hurriedly joined them, with me trailing right behind him. What Pierre had done was lengthen the distance between us and the soldier guarding the rear. The soldier at the head of the column was well out of sight. The other soldier turned his back to us, heading toward the rear of the column to take up his position. As we rounded the bend, we passed a grove of olive trees. Bless them, those beautiful plants that grew to give us olives and oil and—protection.

"Now," Pierre commanded quietly. "Run."

We both jumped to the side and ran among the trees. I didn't feel my legs. I didn't feel anything except that I was moving at great speed when I heard the whirring of a bullet close to me, followed by a ricochet—and then another bullet, and another. One projectile whizzed viciously close to my right ear. Pierre and I zigzagged downhill for what seemed forever before the shooting finally stopped. Yet we kept on running awhile longer. When we felt sure we were a safe distance away, we finally slowed down.

The two of us came upon what looked like a cabbage patch. I'm not sure what it was. Pierre and I dove headlong into it, lying there breathlessly, trying to calm down. My heart was pounding. My lungs felt like they would surely burst. After a spell, I felt Pierre's hand enveloping mine. We squeezed each other's tightly. No words were spoken.

I closed my eyes momentarily, and when I opened them, I saw the most beautiful sight one could imagine: a beautiful, glistening, healthy fat worm. "Hello, you lovely beauty," I sighed. "You have such funny undulations to your body. It's no wonder you like to live in the moist wet earth. It smells divine and is so peaceful and serene. Now that I'm on your level, I can truly understand you better, and I promise I will not step on you when I get up. After all, I'm in your home now, and you don't reject me. So my lovely worm, you who have just made me realize the importance of all creatures, I bid you *adieu*. Whenever I meet one of your cousins, I'll remember you."

I lifted my head and met Pierre's eyes.

"We've made it again, my friend," he said.

I simply nodded, both of us carefully rising to our feet, making sure there were no Germans in sight. Once we felt that the area was clear, we set out for shelter. How I yearned for a piece of fresh meat. I thought about the Doberman.

We walked for a good while through all kinds of vegetation. In the distance, we spied a farm and immediately stopped to surveil the area, making sure that no Germans were around. We waited about an hour then cautiously approached the house. It was getting dark. I felt exhausted and quite cold. My teeth started chattering uncontrollably. The farm was abandoned. What usually happened in this particular area was that there were farmers who lived in the surrounding villages. During the day they would come to work the land, returning home by late afternoon. This seemed to be one of those farms. There was a makeshift shed next to the house. As we approached the structure, we could hear familiar noises, the sounds of chickens talking among themselves.

Pierre's face broke into a big grin. "Coq au vin," he said so happily, disappearing into the shed.

Inside the shed, sheer pandemonium had suddenly erupted. A moment later, Pierre emerged with a chicken in hand. He was holding it by its neck, its head off to a funny angle but still intact. With one swift movement from a sharp implement Pierre had found in a corner, he severed the chicken's head before heading to the house.

We had to force open the door to the house to gain entrance. Inside we found the ever-present rough-hewn furniture and stone fireplace, its chimney floor covered with dead flies. In a chest we found some potatoes, dried figs, a bottle of olive oil and a fair-size piece of bread. WHITE BREAD! It appeared a bit hard but still edible. *We will share this delight, and I won't suffer any stomach pain*, I entertained exultantly.

Pierre must have recognized my silent jubilance. "It's all yours, Antonio," he insisted. "I'm happy for you."

We found some rags and covered the windows, then made a small fire from the unburned wood within the cradle grate. Pierre started to clean the chicken, and I was impressed how he plucked the bird. I went outside to check if the rags prevented any light from being seen. At the same time, I gathered some more wood for the fire. Back inside, I had made a slight adjustment to the window covering, then settled down to the serious business of roasting the chicken. We found a metal rod that served as a spit, and as soon as the fire was going well, we turned the chicken slowly over the flames. It seemed like an eternity had passed, but we eventually began to eat our chicken.

We were so busy eating bird that I didn't realize until the middle of our meal the noisy munching sounds we were making. We retrieved the few potatoes that had been cooking in the hot embers, and now new noises were emanating from our mouths. Munching was mixed with mashing along with an occasional message of thanks.

"Oh, how good you are, Mr. Bird and Mr. Potato," I said in gratitude.

"Ah, I've just burnt my tongue," Pierre blurted out.

"Oh, how I enjoy you, you delectable thing," I went on joyfully.

Our chins were dripping with chicken fat. Pierre looked at me with a big grin when suddenly I heard him release the longest, most devastating earth-shattering belch imaginable. It must have originated from the nails of his toes. His head snapped slightly back—and how we laughed until it hurt. Not to be totally upstaged, I forced a burp, and we roared until the tears were running down our cheeks.

Our hunger and merriment eventually subsided, and after wishing each other good-night, we fell into a deep sleep.

I was awakened the next morning by an indignant voice.

"What in God's name has happened here? Explain your presence. What are these feathers on the floor?"

Pierre got quickly to his feet. I think the rain from yesterday must have further shrunk his pants, exposing his legs high above his ankles. He was an imposing sight to behold. In a booming voice, which he knew how to use quite effectively, he blasted back.

"Are you denying two starving souls the need of some nourishment? Or would you rather be a chicken richer and find us dead in front of your door? Maybe we should have remained outside all night, while eating raw chicken, waiting for you to arrive before asking for your permission to warm ourselves and cook a measly bird. Normally, that would of course be the proper thing to do. But now that you are standing before us, is that truly what you wanted us to do? Speak with your heart as a human being and not as a stingy scoundrel who has no feeling for his fellow man in distress. Go ahead and reveal your choice."

It was a consummate performance. I almost applauded Pierre. I believe he would have graced the Shakespearean stage with great aplomb.

"I'm sorry," the farmer apologized, introducing himself as Federico. "I didn't realize your predicament, gentlemen." He paused and looked at us intently. "Are you *il Professore*, and you the English spy with the radio?"

"I am not a spy," I stated emphatically.

"Oh, don't worry, my mouth is like the grave and the secret is buried deep within."

I once again saw the futility of denial.

"What have you heard on the radio recently?" Federico inquired.

"I really can't say," I stated truthfully yet ambiguously.

"Please tell me how the war is progressing," he practically begged.

"All right, but please keep it under your hat."

"As the Madonna is my witness. Whatever I hear is buried."

I stepped close to the farmer and all but whispered in his ear. "The Allies have infiltrated through a German line: a line that will serve as a first line of offense. The soldiers look like the local farmers and speak the same dialect. That's all I can tell you for now, except for one more thing. There is definitely a movement occurring that will speed up the operation within the next few weeks." I had almost convinced myself. I stepped back from the man.

The farmer's face folded into a big smile, revealing a significant gap between his teeth. "My wife will join us soon," he said. "She is with the donkey. You must stay with us to eat spaghetti. She's bringing white flour. I hope you will forgive me for having thought that you were using my home for dishonorable reasons."

A bosomy woman carrying a large basket on her head appeared in the doorway.

"Rosa, this is the English spy and *il Professore*."

"It gives me great pleasure," she replied, looking down and around at the mess.

"Pleasure is ours," Pierre politely responded.

"I heard you stayed with Martino and Maria for a while," she said. "She and I are related. Her cousin's father's son, who comes from Campoli, and my husband's granddaughter, who is the second wife from the first marriage, are married and now live near Atina."

I didn't understand all those distant relationships, but then I seldom do. All I knew was that everybody was somehow related to one another.

Pierre and I cleaned the floor of the mess we made, repaired the door that we had forced open the day before when we entered the couple's home, then washed up as best we could from all the mud and dust we collected.

Like most farmers, they were endowed with *anima e cuore*: soul and heart, reminding me of an oyster: a rough exterior but with soft and sensitive innards.

In the afternoon, Pierre and I helped Federico and Rosa work their land. For supper we all enjoyed homemade spaghetti with cheese. How I loved that dish. I almost drank it. One chew, two chews and swallow. Wonderful. That evening we were invited to stay while Rosa and Federico went back to the village to spend the night.

We stayed for five days before feeling that we should move on, not wishing to strain the hospitality of our hosts. We finally bid them farewell. It was as if we were close family going off to some faraway land. The couple showed great emotion in the moment we were about to leave. Again, I saw the sensitive side of the oyster. They truly cared for us. Rosa put together two makeshift rucksacks made from burlap, sending us off with a sincere hug. Inside each bag, Pierre and I later found large pieces of white bread and a big hunk of dried goat cheese.

CHAPTER THIRTEEN

Pierre and I roamed the area and eventually learned that groups of people attempting to cross the front lines were still being captured by the Germans and sent to Sora before being shipped off to an undisclosed location. We never found out where or what had happened to them.

I was running an errand for a farmer where Pierre and I were staying, prudently keeping to the area lest I be suspected by the Germans of heading toward the front lines. I saw a German soldier walking on a path just up ahead of me. Adjoining the pathway was a section of land being worked by a farmer handling a spade. Approximately half a mile away was a German camp that was camouflaged with netting. As I continued along, I heard the familiar sound of a canon's projectile boring through the air. As the missile fell and exploded, it made a massive billow of white phosphorous smoke.

The bombing came from the front lines, and the

phosphorous clouds of smoke served to zero in on the German target, or so it seemed. However, the next bomb exploded close to the three of us, away from the German encampment. The irony would be that one of those bombs would fall on top of my head, and I'd be killed by the Allies, I told myself.

"Hey, dummies; you're aiming the wrong way," I said under my breath as I dove headfirst into a trench filled with vegetation. So did the German soldier who had been walking ahead of me. I lifted my head a fraction and shouted to the farmer to get down on the ground.

He simply leaned on his spade and, with a big smile, said, "We are all in the hands of God."

Bombs started raining all around us. I ducked my head and tucked my body tightly to the trench. Then as suddenly as the bombing had started, it abruptly stopped. Not taking any chances, I cautiously raised my head after having waited several minutes. The first thing I did was look for the farmer. He was no more. Pieces of his clothing were all that were visible. He was now truly in the hands of God. I felt terrible. I looked around and saw uprooted olive trees; others with partially severed branches hanging askew; still other trees lay severed by shrapnel.

For some reason, my swelling face seemed as if it were on fire. I figured I had jumped into a trench filled with poisonous growth, which proved to be the case. I saw the German getting out of a trench not far from me. He looked in my direction.

"That's the rotten Americans. You see for yourselves, now, who your friends are," he said in German.

I merely shrugged uncomprehendingly. His face was swelling, too, rather severely. I climbed cautiously out of the trench but kept close by should I need to disappear into the earth like Mr. Worm.

When I returned from my errand, Pierre found me with my eyes seemingly sealed. My face had swollen out of proportion. We were staying in the barn of a farmer. Pierre administered cold compresses, which helped relieve the terrible itch.

"Better to have a fat face than wear the death mask, my dear friend," he swore.

I couldn't agree with him more. As if by some miracle, the swelling subsided and was gone the following day.

"As it turned out, you were in the middle of a

deadly bombing raid yesterday," Pierre said, "and I feel in my bones that this is an undeniable sign of the beginning of the end for the German swine."

I agreed with Pierre wholeheartedly. We looked around the village square and saw no sign of any Germans. For whatever reason, we decided to get a haircut, which took place in the open square. I don't know how any barber had the courage to cut hair out in the open, but one barber was doing exactly that. Pierre and I had our beards shaved when we could. We approached the barber who was finishing up cutting the hair of the mayor's son, Carlo, whom we knew fairly well. Surrounding us were several locals, sunning themselves, chewing on black cigars and relaxing. It was more than a respite from the constant strain. Hope was in the air— palpable and positive expectation was on the horizon.

"Hey, *Professore*," the barber greeted Pierre. "How is everything going?" As the mayor's son left the chair, he approached us with a concerned look.

"Pierre, Antonio, I have some very important news for you. See me at my house at five o'clock."

We said we would come by. With that, Carlo left. Pierre took his place in the barber chair.

After the barber finished cutting Pierre's hair, the

man began to shave his beard. When he was halfway finished, a German officer flanked by two orderlies appeared. They approached the barber chair.

"You filthy dog, move your ass out of that chair," the officer said in German.

Pierre needed no translation; however, he wasn't fast enough for the officer, who grabbed him by an ear and pulled him out of the chair with only half his beard shaved.

Pierre's face was beet red, but whatever hatred was welling up inside of him remained under control. He walked over to me while the officer took the seat. The Germans had their own barbers, so I couldn't understand why the officer had to have his hair cut here.

"What did he say to me?" Pierre asked quietly.

I told him. He still didn't display any emotion. When the officer finally had his hair cut, he stood, threw some insults our way then left with the two orderlies. Pierre returned to the chair, and the barber finished shaving him. I was next and took a seat. All the while, the local folks just sat there and said nothing. They were wise to keep silent. What could they do? When the barber finished, Pierre and I left the square.

"How I so hate those Germans, Antonio."

It was the way Pierre said those words that made me feel good to be his friend. Our pride was hurt, but we were alive.

"Let's go see what Carlo wants," he said.

We walked quietly, side by side. Pierre always took very long strides. Although I was four inches taller, I had difficulty keeping up with him. Through the narrow streets we walked until we came to Carlo's house. We made sure that no Germans were in sight before entering.

Carlo was a man of about twenty-five, recently the father of a baby who was sitting on his lap. He was feeding the child and told us to take a seat. His wife was busy in the kitchen.

"Let me get right to the point," Carlo began. "My father, who you're well-aware is the mayor, was asked to cooperate with the Germans by letting them know where escaped English and American prisoners of war may be staying in the area. Of course, he is not going to do any such thing. Now, what's important for you to know is . . . ." he turned to his wife who entered the room. "Take the baby, please," he said, handing both the bottle and child over to its mother. Carlo stood, walked over to a closet and took out a map. "You see this area?" He made a circular motion over a particular section. "The Germans are going to make a thorough search by encompassing it from this side, where we are situated now. It will take them about two days to cover the area to the opposite side. They claim that an organization of military personnel, unfriendly to them, have created havoc, and they want to stop them cold by rounding up all the English and Americans. I do not think they will be too selective. They referred to one particular assault on their truck convoy some weeks back, where they said they were attacked from the mountains by a few hundred people."

"Did they say where the attack took place?" I asked.

"Yes, right here," Carlo indicated, pointing to the area that we knew so well. "Many German soldiers and several officers died there."

Pierre and I looked at each other, and I saw the iciness fixed upon his face since the incident at the public square earlier suddenly melt away, replaced by a warm glow. His eyes revealed the sign of satisfaction.

"So, I think it in your best interest to leave as soon as you can and head for Capistrello, or Avezzano," Carlo suggested. "There will be a house-to-house search starting tomorrow."

"Then we must leave now," Pierre decided.

"I think so, too," said Carlo. "But before you go, will you please do me the honor of sharing a meal with us. Yes?"

We ate very quietly, thanking Carlo and his wife profusely for the food and information. The couple was endangering themselves, for anyone who provided us with food or shelter would be considered harboring enemies as far as the Germans were now concerned. We finished our meal and bid those two brave folks good-bye.

Cautiously, we exited their home and made our way to the farmer's barn where we collected a few belongings. We waited until it grew dark.

"We go, now, Antonio. We have a full moon, and the sooner we start the better."

Pierre and I thanked the farmer then headed out. We heard the big guns barking loudly. I felt frustrated. It seems that whenever we were close to liberation, something or someone always intervened, somehow deciding that it wasn't yet time for me to have my most magnificent meal or delicious lady. I looked to the moon for guidance.

"You up there with the smiling face. When are you going to do something about our suffering? Sure you're smiling because you don't have to show any documents to the shitheads down here. So you stay up there and keep on smiling. You're the only one who seems to be eternally happy."

Pierre and I had considerably extended the distance between us and the farmer's village, yet we knew that we still had a tough trek over mountainous terrain ahead of us. So we didn't talk, we just walked steadily into the night while other people were sleeping in their warm beds and having intimate relationships that I could only dream about.

We trudged through the night like hunted animals. I was getting madder by the minute. *You bastards who take great satisfaction in fearful faces. You dogs who decide which human beings will live or die. You door smashers. You who have the audacity to publicly proclaim yourselves the only race worthy of life and liberty. You book burners. You are revealing yourselves before the world forever as mass murderers. I will fight you with every square inch of my body and spirit. I will fight your injustices and your cruelty. Bastards that you are.*

Pierre turned around. "Hey, what's the matter, Antonio?" He must have sensed my emotional upheaval because he put a protective arm around my shoulder. "It's all right, my good friend. Take it easy. We'll make it."

He wiped the sweat from my brow. "Easy now, my loyal companion. Easy does it."

"I'll be all right," I said. "Let's continue."

We walked on and on for hours, cursing the steep inclines and blessing the downward slopes. The ropes of the rucksack were cutting deep into my shoulders. I thought I would never reach the top of a mountain. My feet felt as if they were a hundred pounds each. My body was bent forward to counteract the weight upon my shoulders. *One more step and I'll drop and sleep for a whole week,* I swore. I took another step, promising myself that I'd stop. *My pumping heart is going to burst open. Then I shall surely sleep. I can't take it anymore. I can't go on. This is the end. I'm going to lie down.* I took another step. My breath was wheezing in and out.

"I can't go on, Pierre," I declared. "This is where I stop. I've had it."

Pierre turned around, hooked a hand under one of the rucksack ropes, removing it from my shoulder. He unhooked the other. I didn't have the strength to protest. Without saying a word, he once again slung the burlap bag atop his own and continued upward.

I just didn't possess the physical stamina that Pierre had. He had such energy that left me bewildered.

With the weight of the cutting ropes off my shoulders, I somehow managed to forge ahead. We continued walking through the night.

At dawn we came upon an empty sheep shed. All I remember was entering it through a rickety door. When I woke up, I was lying with my face in dry droppings.

"Let's go, Antonio. Up you go." Pierre was shaking my shoulder.

The two of us crawled painfully out of the shed. The sun was in its eight o'clock position, so I figured we must have slept less than three hours. We retrieved a piece of dried sausage and goat cheese, and off again we went, walking the whole day but with frequent intervals of rest. By nightfall we reached a small village, which we later learned was Santa Maria. We sought shelter along the outskirts. It was either that or drop in our tracks and sleep right there when we saw a building in the distance. Together, we plodded along toward it. After closer investigation, it turned out to be a school of sorts. We entered the premises by forcing open a window, finding a room lined with cots. However, no one was in them. I thought perhaps that the cots were there for the children to take a nap during the day. I set down the rucksack, removed my boots, and was asleep before my head hit the canvas cot.

I don't know how long Pierre and I slept before we were awakened by stomping sounds. I just couldn't open my eyes. Then something hard poked me in the ribs. "*Aufstehen.*"

My eyes suddenly popped open and focused on a German soldier pointing the muzzle of his rifle at my head. Pierre and I were surrounded by children and presumably their teacher, a woman of about fifty. Another soldier was getting Pierre up in the same harsh manner.

"What's happening?" I asked the woman for lack of anything better to say.

The woman smirked before explaining. "Some partisans blew up a power station in the vicinity, and they are looking for the culprit . . . or culprits," she added glumly.

What dumb luck, I thought. To be caught for something with which we had nothing to do. The soldiers motioned for us to follow them. Pierre and I put on our footwear, picked up our rucksacks, then headed out to the street.

It was a bright day. The kids were following us, making silly remarks, giggling and behaving like children do; nothing more, nothing less. But I felt as though I was on display, like an exploited animal exposed to an audience for the price of admission. The two soldiers walked in back of us, pointing the way with rifle barrels. After a few minutes, we arrived at a spacious building that was unmistakably German headquarters. A large red flag flaunting a black swastika hung high above the entrance.

We were led to a room. One soldier left while the other kept watch over us. A few minutes later the other soldier returned with an officer. He had a crew cut and wore very round glasses. His uniform was immaculate. I studied his face carefully, like he was studying mine. Pierre and I looked the part we played, two refugee peasants trying to get home to our families. We would act very dumb and submissive.

The officer slowly and deliberately seated himself before picking up a stack of papers from his desk, tapping them up and down to straighten the edges evenly.

My mouth felt like dry cardboard; the beat of my heart resounded in my ears. Without lifting his eyes, he quietly spoke to us in English. "I know that you are English spies."

I felt sick to my stomach, squeezing the cheeks of

my buttocks together.

"I know that you were sent here to sabotage our military operations, to impede our movements, to play havoc among our military personnel."

Now, I was really squeezing.

"And I also know that you are the ones responsible for blowing up the power station at Santa Maria." Like a wild cat, he sprung from his seat, the chair clattering to the floor. The officer smashed both fists upon the table. "Confess immediately, or you'll be shot without delay!" he screamed.

While interlocking my fingers and bending slightly at the knees, I replied in Italian. "We are refugees from the south, seeking protection with the Germans in order to escape the marauding Americans. This is my uncle who is mentally retarded, and I have to take care of him. He is shell shocked, and I want to take him to a hospital. We are innocent farmers."

Out of the corner of my eyes, I saw that Pierre had assumed an idiotic look. His shoulders drooped excessively, and he stood hunched slightly forward. A deadly silence prevailed.

The officer picked up the chair, sat back down,

adjusted his glasses then fidgeted with the pile of papers. He now spoke to us in German. "Since it is known to me that you are both German deserters, I can guarantee that you will have to pay dearly if you don't admit immediately that you have turned your backs on the fatherland, you stinking foul dogs. Confess!" There went the chair again.

Mustering a modicum of courage, I thought—not fought—how to tackle this megalomaniac. *Don't fight it, feed it. He wants power? Then give it to him.* I fell on my knees and held Pierre by the hand, the other hand outstretched toward the bastard. Make sure he understands the first word because he doesn't speak or understand Italian. Enunciate each syllable.

"*Gen·er·ale!*"

Up upon his toes he went, reminding me of someone I knew in Barcelonnette. The lieutenant's chest swelled as he threw a glance at the picture of Hitler hanging on the wall.

"Oh, my *Generale*," I continued in Italian. "I don't know what you want with us poor farmers." I was truly animated. "Please help us to rejoin our families. Please, I beg your lordship." Pierre's hand felt like a deflated sausage in mine. What a performance. As for my own performance, it seemed to be working.

The lieutenant called for an orderly and told him to take us to be interrogated at Avezzano. I got up off my knees. We were gestured toward the door, and I led Pierre by the hand outside to a waiting truck. Two soldiers motioned for us to enter the back of the vehicle. As Pierre and I stepped up and in, I saw the stares and heard the voices of the villagers. I overheard someone in the crowd referring to the two of us.

"Yes, the taller one; he's an English spy."

The ride was a very short one. We arrived at a huge building that looked like a fort. The front section of the walled structure was, in fact, a prison. I felt sick to my stomach again. As a child, I used to watch insects, and then put them in a glass jar. I felt exactly like one of those creatures. Pierre maintained the look of complete helplessness. We were escorted through a large door that closed behind us with a hollow sounding thud. We were then led through a maze of corridors and put into a filthy, foul-smelling cell. Pierre and I sat down on a large bench.

"Where did you get the brilliant idea of turning me into an idiot?" he asked.

"I don't know."

"Never mind. I think it was a good one, so don't fret. We'll get out of this predicament, too. You'll see."

Where did this man, in the face of sheer and constant danger, get his cocky assurance and self-confidence? We sat there for about two hours when a soldier opened the door and motioned us outside. We followed him, the sound of his thumping boots resounding along the cold corridors. Pierre and I looked at each other, exchanging a knowing glance. It seemed as if the soldier suddenly read our thoughts. He paused and motioned us to walk ahead of him. I thought perhaps he might be new on the job, a temporary replacement. Regardless, we wouldn't have been able to do anything because there were too many locked doors between us and the outside. We'd be fumbling with keys and probably wind up in the arms of a small army of men.

We walked by a long window lined with bars. Outside on the ledge sat a little bird, holding its head to one side as if studying us. Oh, how I wished to be in its place, being able to spread my wings and fly away to freedom.

We came to a door, and the soldier opened it widely, ushering us inside. The room had a very large table placed in the center. Behind it sat a German officer with black bushy eyebrows; not a single hair on his head.

Next to the officer sat Gustavo.

The feeling that I had the moment I saw him I never experienced the rest of my life. The closest I can come to describing the sensation was as if someone had driven a wedge that penetrated my skull, then traveled straight down the center of my being, separating everything into two equal parts, and I do mean everything. I was emotionally severed. There wasn't the slightest sign from Gustavo that he recognized either Pierre or me. Likewise, neither Pierre nor I communicated any recognition.

Our interrogation was conducted by Gustavo, who, acting as a translator for the soldier standing beside him, asked me in Italian to show him our documentation. I handed Gustavo my document, explaining that the reason Pierre didn't have anything on him was because the barbarous Americans bombed our farm and most of our personal belongings were destroyed.

"Where were you going when you were apprehended by the authorities?" Gustavo inquired.

"We were in the process of escaping from the Americans."

"What do you know of the explosion of the power station in Santa Maria?"

Pierre and I looked at each other. "What power station?" I asked him with genuine innocence.

The interrogation went on for approximately ten minutes: the German soldier probing, Gustavo translating from German to Italian. Lastly, we were asked if we had ever been arrested by the German authorities.

"Us? No, never. Of course not."

As Gustavo translated, I somehow felt that we were safe for the moment.

A load of questions had certainly popped into my own head. How did Gustavo manage to talk himself into this position of translator after having been arrested and marched off to Sora? What was the reason behind his behavior? He could be shot on the spot for not revealing what he knew about Pierre and me. Who was he really? Perhaps *Gustavo* was a German spy? Wouldn't that be ironic? I entertained. Then I considered the possibility that he may have forgotten about us. Maybe all the terrible things that had happened to him had warped his memory. Had he forgotten that some sixty of us had been arrested near Cassino, marched off in single file to Sora? Did he not remember that Pierre and I escaped into the olive trees? There were all kinds of questions and possible scenarios running through my mind.

Pierre stood limply by my side.

"What happened to your uncle?" Gustavo inquired.

"Oh, he had typhus, and for all I know he may still have it," I said with childish innocence, recalling the mother and daughter who had saved my life back in Rome with that same story.

Gustavo translated.

Suddenly, the furrows of the soldier's forehead deepened, and his face flushed.

That was the end of our interrogation. An orderly was called, and we were immediately led back to our cell. The sickening sound of its solid steel door clanged closed behind us.

Pierre had the same questions and possible explanations concerning Gustavo's behavior as I had entertained. We considered our predicament and possibilities of escape. In spite of Pierre's positive outlook, our situation seemed rather bleak. Our discussion was interrupted by someone fidgeting with the key in the cell door.

As the door opened, Gustavo appeared with an orderly behind him. He had a big smile on his face, and in his hand he held a slip of paper.

"Well, gentlemen, this is your release from prison, which you will submit to the guards at the outside gate.

And this paper," he retrieved another from his pocket, "will authorize you to render yourselves to a refugee camp near Celano. Good luck to you both." He turned to Pierre. "I hope that you get rid of all the residuals of your typhus." His smile grew bigger. Gustavo stepped very close to me and, in *sotto voce*, instructed, "If you want to play the part of an Italian, work harder to improve your accent. Come."

Pierre and I stepped from the cell and followed Gustavo down another long corridor before having the orderly escort us outside. Gustavo turned and faced me for a final time.

"Thank you for the figs and your compassion," he concluded with a wink and a warm smile.

Two minutes later we were breathing fresh air again. We had no intention of rendering or surrendering ourselves to anyone but the Americans.

CHAPTER FOURTEEN

Pierre and I wanted to run instead of walk before anyone changed their minds about having released us. However, we both thought better of it. We grinned at one another, and I thought to myself, *Pierre what a beautiful face you posses; and your teeth are like pearls.* Of course, his teeth were as black as tar, but I realized at a relatively early age that it was an inner beauty that makes a human being shine brightly.

I recalled walking in the park in Antwerp as a youngster when I heard one little girl say to another, "Oh, boy, you really look ugly." And the other girl replied, "Do you think I want to be?" In that moment, she became beautiful to me, whereas the other girl, who made the infantile remark, wearing a beautiful petticoat and ribbons in her hair that framed a comely face, had turned truly ugly. So, too, my friend Pierre was beautiful because he truly *was* within.

We walked along a country road until we came to a

cluster of houses. As Pierre and I approached an opening between two dwellings, we entered the small alley and grabbed each other by the shoulders. We danced the tarantella and a Cossack Victory Dance. Up and down we jumped, legs kicking big holes in the air as we uttered oohs and ahs mixed among delicious hysterical laughter when suddenly something erupted. I heard a big noise from somewhere, but I didn't know what it was. Pierre stood stock-still. His face had taken on an expression of dramatic astonishment as he stood there motionless. I stopped my dancing and was bewildered by what had happened. But what did happen?

Pierre turned and said to me, very seriously, "My dear friend. I just shit in my pants."

I came close to dying from laughter, inhaling a single gulp of air that sent my body reeling backward before doubling over forward, expelling the air that filled my lungs, my stomach, my knee caps and toes. The air kept on coming out, but nothing came back in. I felt sure that my tonsils were going to come rolling out and drop to the ground. The expelling stream of air was just one big H-HHHaaaaa. For the life of me, I just could not catch my breath. Still, I had the presence of mind to realize it would prove the dumbest thing I've done to date to die from one big H-HHHaaaaa than it would be to die in the heat of battle. Pierre elaborated in earnest that he had a load in his pants. Surely I would die there on the spot. Somehow I managed to crank the upper part of my body to a vertical position, miraculously wheezing precious air back into my lungs.

As I lifted my head, I saw Pierre walking off into a field in a kind of duck waddle, his feet wide apart while clutching on to his backside. This was too much. I nearly fell down. I was leaning against the wall of one of the houses for support. Finally, I let loose a peal of laughter that must have sounded like a moose having an orgasm as I slowly sank to the ground—spent.

As I was trying to compose myself, there appeared a farmer from around the corner. The man had a concerned look on his face. "Are you sick?" he asked.

"Oh, no. Quite the contrary. I'm very happy. What happened was that my friend and I were—I mean, my friend and I were so happy that he—well, let's just say that something very funny happened. I had a good laugh while my friend had a good . . . . Oh, let me get up."

The farmer lent me a hand. "They call me Franco," he said.

"Antonio is my name, and my friend, who ought to

show up fairly soon, is Pierre."

"Are you per chance the English spy and he *il Professore*?"

Our reputation seemed to precede us, and by now I had gotten used to it. Surprisingly, I felt a sense of enjoyment. No more denying it. Just try to get something into our bellies, I told myself. I ran the moniker through my mind. *La Spia Inglese.* It sounded like a line from an opera. I sang it mentally to note which way it would sound more dramatic. It should definitely be sung by a dark, menacing baritone like Scarpia in *Tosca.*

"Were you just coming out from jail?" he questioned.

I looked down surprisingly at the short man but said nothing.

The farmer scratched the stubble upon his hollow face, standing there in ill-fitting clothes. "Oh, I saw you coming from there. Usually, they ride their prisoners away in trucks. It's rare to see someone walking out of there. You must have powerful connections on the inside. Yes?"

I wanted to squeeze all the enjoyment I could out of my answer. "Yes, I do."

The farmer's eyes squinted to narrow slits, and at the same time his mouth displayed four teeth on top and two on the bottom. "Bravo, bravo!" he exclaimed. "It pleases me to hear that you have such far-reaching connections."

We stayed and chatted while waiting for Pierre to return. When he finally appeared in the distance, he seemed to have changed somewhat. Gone was his steady stride. Instead, there was a slow sort of shuffle to his walk, along with a noticeable slouch across his narrow shoulders. It seemed that a part of his manhood had disappeared in his pants. No questions as to where he washed his underwear would I ask. No wisecracks or jokes would I make, I promised myself. I must not cause my friend a moment of embarrassment. I'll just make believe nothing happened, I swore.

"Hey, Pierre. Meet my new friend, Franco," I said with a warm, sincere smile.

Pierre paused for a second and studied the farmer's features. "Franco, do you have family in Val di Comino?" Pierre asked the little man.

"Yes, I do," Franco answered with a degree of surprise.

"Do the names Martino and Maria mean anything

to you?" Pierre pressed

"Sure, Martino is my brother."

Only then did I recognize the similarity. "How did you know?" I asked Pierre.

"There was that picture upstairs on the wall above your bed."

"Oh, yes. Now I remember." And with that realization, I remembered, too, Maria's floating bosom.

"Come with me to my house," Franco invited. "We don't have much, but we'll be able to find you both something to eat. Maybe some spaghetti."

We followed Franco through a typical rural village. As we passed one particular house, the curtain was moved aside and the painted face of a woman with a pointed chin appeared, making suggestive motions with her head and eyes.

"Bad woman," Franco explained. "German soldiers visit her often, and right across the street from my own house. It's a disgrace. And to think that I went to her christening. This war has turned everything upside down. But the time will come when everything will be straightened out, and justice will prevail. We must have faith in Santa Maria."

Franco, like most of the farmers, was a deeply devout man, and I respected his beliefs.

The houses stood very close together. If I were to extend both arms out to either side, I could practically touch the adjacent walls. We climbed five crudely-built stone steps, turned right along a porch way then entered the all-too-familiar arrangement of rooms, along with the ever-present order of burned, dead wood from the fireplace.

"This is Margherita, my wife," Franco announced. "Margherita, these men are none other than the English spy and *il Professore*. Sit down, gentlemen, please. Margherita will make something to eat. You know, Margherita, the spy and *il professore* were just released from the jail. They have connections there; that's why they got out."

The woman moved cautiously across the room. Then with a calm voice she spoke. "You can stay one night only. Then you must leave." She turned away to go prepare something for us to eat.

"Margherita! One night?" The farmer looked at us, then lifted his shoulders in a gesture of helplessness.

I understood the woman's fear of harboring people like us.

"Tomorrow is a big holiday, and we have a lot to prepare," Franco said in defense of his wife's firm decision. "The Feast of San Gennaro requires a lot of work. Have you heard anything of the progress of the war?" our host inquired, having switched gears abruptly.

Pierre unfolded fictitious details about paratroopers and battalions and secret plans that were being drawn up by the high command of the Allied forces.

The farmer was elated. "You have to be careful around here because a German garrison has stationed itself just outside of town," he warned.

"What does it consist of?" Pierre asked.

"A lot of trucks—maybe fifty—and many soldiers. They just came back from the front. I saw them transporting a whole bunch of their wounded. There seems to be a lot more shooting recently. More so than usual."

A whole bunch of wounded German soldiers, I framed in my mind. I liked that picture, and so did Pierre.

"Come, I show you where you sleep tonight."

We went back outside and down the stone steps. Adjacent to the house was a large barn filled with the usual farm tools. Piled high in one corner of the space was a heap of corn husks. In another corner was a mound of dried corn leaves.

"This is all I can offer you tonight," Franco said. "I'm sorry. My Margherita is a good woman. I hope you understand."

"Don't worry about a thing, Franco," I assured him. "We understand perfectly well. I would appreciate it, though, if you could provide us with some water so that we could wash up a bit."

"I'll fetch you some hot water in a bucket."

An hour later, Pierre and I washed our bodies then laundered our ragged clothing with the same water. If I could only get rid of these damn crab lice, I complained. They had nestled themselves so firmly in my pubic hair that there was just no way of getting rid of them. I was as thin as a reed, and I often wondered what I had to offer these damn creatures. After having dressed in our wrinkled, wrung-out clothing, we went back to the house.

Margherita had prepared a big bowl of spaghetti and white beans. The hours passed rapidly. Night had fallen, and Pierre excused himself, deciding to go to sleep. I remained behind, talking to Franco for a spell before leaving to join Pierre.

It was a clear night, and the moon showed itself in golden splendor. I stepped outside, turned and headed toward the steps. I heard Franco lock the door behind me. I inhaled deeply while looking up at the stars. I stood there for a while, when across the street the woman with the painted face and pointed chin suddenly opened her front door. From behind the woman, out stepped a German soldier. He saw me standing there, and I froze. She closed the door behind him. The soldier studied me for a full twenty seconds. Very slowly he started walking toward me when I suddenly realized that it was way past curfew. The soldier was mumbling something under his breath while swaying as he crossed the street. My mind was a muddling mess before it registered that the man was drunk. He was practically in my face. I could smell the alcohol on his breath and now understood what he was saying. He was in a quiet rage, climbing clumsily to the top of the steps as I moved back against the wall. I could go no further.

"You filthy swine dog," he muttered. "You think you can get away with anything you like while I burn my ass off at the front." He took a final step, holding on to the wall. "I'll show you bastards who's boss around here. You think I don't know you're laughing at me behind my back, making fun of us."

He reached for my throat, and I acted instinctively —no thinking, debating, or weighing of consequences. I hooked my right leg in back of his, and with one swift motion, pushed him backward—hard. He hit the wall with a sudden thud and just stood there. There was no sign of movement. His head was sloped at a queer position. I stepped closer, realizing what had happened. A trickle of blood lined the soldier's collar. Embedded at the base his skull was a spike that the family used to hang religious pictures during festivals. The impaled German soldier stood there . . . stone-cold dead.

I relieved him of his weapons, a rifle and pistol, then promptly entered the barn where Pierre was sound asleep. I woke him up and proceeded to tell him what had happened. He immediately got up and went outside to see for himself. Without a moment's deliberation, Pierre firmly decided. "We have to go, now! But first, go and tell Franco what happened and to get rid of the body and to wash up the blood. If anyone comes looking for that Nazi, tell Franco to say he heard a violent argument erupt across the street. We don't want him blamed for this."

Pierre went back to the barn and quickly collected our belongings, and I told Franco what had just occurred. Instead of heading north to the refugee camp, we immediately headed south into the mountains. I was very shaken by the whole experience, and Pierre must have picked up on it because he kept talking about the most senseless and trivial subjects. Occasionally, he succeeded in diverting my thoughts from the recent event.

"So my Aunt Germaine came home with a basket full of strawberries instead of jam," Pierre went on nonsensically. "Well, I want you to guess what she might have decided to do with them. Go ahead and guess."

"I don't know," I answered.

"Come on, make an effort."

"Uh, she ate them all up?"

"Oh, boy, are you silly. Come on, try again. You're allowed two more guesses."

"She gave them all away."

I figured Pierre had grown impatient because he didn't give me time for a final guess. "She made compote from those darling berries. Can you imagine?"

Later, he tired of describing the lace on the curtains in his grandmother's living room.

"Thank you, Pierre. I appreciate your concern. I'll be all right."

He nodded unconvincingly, and we trudged along the narrow mountain paths. Very seldom did we encounter Germans on these mountain trails, which gave us relief to a large extent. The problem was that we always had to go back to the more cultivated areas of the villages for food. That was the sole reason we would expose ourselves to potential danger, either from the Germans or, unfortunately and ironically, the Allies, who occasionally tried to pepper the Germans with field artillery and, more often than not, would miss the enemy by a considerable margin, remarkably succeeding in uprooting old trees and making dust of boulders. The side of the mountain we now traversed was on the opposite side that had offered a birds-eye view of the valley. However, from our present vantage point, the valley below was invisible, affording us protection for when we descended into its depth. A section of the valley formed a gentle serpentine-like curvature that disappeared when viewed from above the craggy precipice.

Pierre stopped suddenly. "Do you hear?"

For a moment I didn't know what he was talking about. Then I heard the distant humming of a plane. We both turned, and from a distance we saw a plane appearing around a bend, followed by another aircraft—

then another, and another. Four planes. *Friend or foe?* I wondered. They were thirty to forty feet below us when Pierre exclaimed, "Spitfires!" My heart started pumping faster and faster. The planes came closer, and the roar of the engines filled the valley. The first plane was near enough to discern the pilot. Pierre and I started jumping up and down to get their attention. The aircraft passed without the pilot noticing us. Maybe the second one will see us, I prayed. I must really make a greater effort this time. *Come on, Sam, wave harder. Shout! That's it, shout; they may hear you.*

The second plane approached. "Stop, stop, we're here. Up here." I could see the young-looking face of the pilot, his countenance set in a grim stare, looking straight ahead and following the path of the first plane. *Two more planes, Sam, and that's it.* The third plane came even closer. I waved, making huge circles in the air. Pierre was doing the same. We were jumping up and down like marionettes. "Over here, to your right, up here," I shouted. "Turn your head. Look over here . . . please." He slid right by us, following his companions.

The fourth plane was fast approaching. *All right, Sam, your last chance. This is final. If this guy doesn't see you, you'll probably rot among these mountains. You'll never get out. Never!* "Look this way, please, you stupid bastard," I screamed. "Over here to your right. Look, look, please, you son of a bitch. Look to your goddamn right. Oh, God, please." We were both jumping like madmen. Suddenly, he saw us. He turned his head to his right, looked straight at us, and his austere features changed into a smile. He winked at us and waved.

"He's waving at us, Pierre. Look, he's looking straight at us—" and then he was gone.

The turbulence from the aircraft had dislodged a rock, which rolled down the side of the mountain, taking with it other rocks along the way. The mass of stone crashed into the abyss below, and we were alone again. The drone of the engines gradually faded, followed by their silence. I was in a sweat. We both sat down, panting heavily before falling silent, too. After a time, we got up and continued our journey.

For a week we moved through the countryside, avoiding German installations, keeping to the narrow paths, away from the roads. We stopped at nearby farms for a few days; we worked, ate and invented news. We were almost always received with a warm welcome, then moved on to the village of Atina, which we hoped was the approach to Cassino and the Americans.

One early morning during our travels, Pierre said, "There's the road, no more than fifty miles, and all downhill."

I was not at all happy with the view. "And only five miles down the hill, the Germans," I contributed pessimistically.

Pierre refused to be denied. "Tonight we will slither through their lines like snakes."

As he spoke we heard footsteps approaching in the distance. Dropping quickly to the ground, we hurriedly buried our weapons in the loose soil and stones then sat and waited.

A German soldier appeared, looked nervously around as he raised his rifle and pointed it at us. "*Aufstehen, los, papiere.*"

We gave him our papers as I spoke in Italian, employing key words that he would hopefully grasp. "We are farmers trying to get home to Naples by way of a refugee camp. The murderous Americans bombed our home and killed our parents. We came to the Germans for safety."

"*Halt den Mund!* he barked at us.

Off to our left, two British soldiers came cautiously

upon us with their rifles raised and at the ready.

"Hold it right there, Kraut," the taller one ordered. We all froze. "Put that rifle down carefully."

The shorter soldier quickly checked out the immediate area and returned. "Gimme 'em papers," he commanded, grabbing them from the German's hand. He studied the documents for a good moment. "These two are Eye-talian," he said.

Pierre proudly puffed out his scrawny chest in sheer annoyance. "I am French, from Lyon."

"And I am Belgian, from Antwerp," I added.

The taller Brit now nodded with understanding. A Belgian and a Frog," he said.

Pierre glowered at the word Frog.

I pointed eagerly to Pierre and myself. "American prisoners, yes?"

The Brit glared at me. "We are British, Brit-ish. You are prisoners of His Majesty King George the Sixth." His chest puffed up as proudly as Pierre's.

Pierre was a bit crestfallen. "Oh, British, ah, oh, well, good."

The Brit was annoyed. "Oh, good is it! Maybe you

prefer the Krauts?"

Pierre shook his head emphatically. The two of us grinned and hugged one another.

"Quit that now," the Brit said. "Move." And to the other Brit, "Could we get out of here? There must be more Krauts about if this one's here, and I want me tea."

Pierre and I were taken to a British encampment near Naples, where we were politely questioned, as opposed to being interrogated and accepted as refugees—not prisoners.

A British officer came into the room where I sat. Pierre was being questioned in another room. The officer pinned a map on the wall. "Now then, where are the installations you described?"

I pointed to Alvito at Val di Comino, Picinisco, and Cassino. "Here, here and here. This is the area where we were captured, Monte Meta, and taken to headquarters where we were to be transported to Sora, then to an undisclosed location—for disposal. The next morning approximately sixty of us were marched off in single file along a narrow path through the hills, headed toward Sora. Only two soldiers escorted us, one at each end of the column. Pierre and I were in the middle. We came to a sharp bend, and for a moment we were out of sight of the two guards. A quick signal from Pierre, and we ran headlong down the hill through the olive trees that covered the slope. Bullets snapped all around us till we were out of range. We ran forever before collapsing, safe for that moment."

The officer was moved and impressed. "You chaps had quite an adventure. I'm going to note these installations to my report." He removed the maps from the wall and rolled them up. "You have been very helpful. We'll continue this later." He turned and walked out.

Pierre and I were directed to a room where we washed, shaved and were given clean clothes. We sat there reflecting on what was to happen to us next. I had visions of the Brits sending me to England for further processing, wondering if I'd wind up in the Belgian Army. Pierre believed that there was the possibility he'd be sent to serve in the French Foreign Legion. We both laughed at the conceivable irony. Where were the Americans?

"To have come this far to find and fight for the British," I roared. "And now we're just two poor refugees."

Pierre sighed heavily "Well, it's either the French Foreign Legion for me or the stockade if I decline the offer.

I'm not sure which I'll choose. Either way I should be warm and dry and rid of fleas. If I serve faithfully, I'm sure they'll serve me all the meat I wish."

The mere talk and thought of food, especially meat, had us realize that we were both famished. "Wait here," I told Pierre.

I left the room and disappeared around the corridor to locate the kitchen area. I was actually taking food from the kitchen and hiding it in my clothes just in case the Germans came back. One of the officers saw me. He knew what I was doing. The man came over and gently put his hand upon my shoulder.

"Now, now, matie," he said softly, "You're safe here. No need to steal any food."

Imagine if he were a German soldier. I would have been shot where I stood. I returned to the room with a dish piled high with biscuits and a thermos of tea.

"This is just for starters, mate," I said playfully to Pierre. "They're feeding us a real honest-to-goodness meal of roasted chicken with all the trimmings later tonight."

Pierre politely took and put the dish and thermos aside, looking up at me with a big smile. "Do you have any idea what a meal is without wine, my very good friend?"

I simply shook my head.

"Just food, Antonio, my friend. Just food. Do you recall my promising you a magnificent meal when we got out of that hell?"

I nodded in the affirmative.

"We're leaving this camp for a few hours. One of the pilots who had spotted us later radioed in that information. A British officer has made arrangements for us to go into the city on some sort of pretext. Don't ask any questions, and say nothing to anyone. Just follow me."

I felt there was something quite strange in this so-called arrangement.

CHAPTER FIFTEEN

B ack in our room later that evening, Pierre and I sat laughing hysterically.

"I don't think I'll ever forget the look on the waiter's face when you handed him back the check," I roared. "You practically forced me into ordering all those fancy appetizers, along with two bottles of wine, soup, salad, entrée and dessert—at one of the finest restaurants in Naples, no less. Then when he returned with the maître d', both of them *insisting* that you pay the bill—" another surge of laughter overcame me, "—you told them—" I gasped for air.

"I told him to send the bill to Mussolini," Pierre repeated with utmost satisfaction.

I could barely catch my breath.

"Well, did they really expect me to pay for it?" Pierre continued. "That clochard and his cronies made big bucks catering to the Germans through black-market operations, the British officer had assured me, while you and I were starving and freezing in the mountains."

A bit drunk, the two of us rose and flung our arms around each other. In the morning, surprisingly, an orderly came for Pierre and escorted him outside to a waiting van. He seemed in good spirits. We said our good-byes, and I was told that Pierre was being sent to Caluire-et-Cuire, a commune just north of Lyon. From there, he was supposedly going home.

It had been two years from the time I left Belgium in 1942.

Shortly after the war, with the help of friends in Europe, I searched high and low for Pierre, starting in Lyon, Caluire-et-Cuire, and even the French Foreign Legion, but could find no trace of him. There wasn't a Pierre Francois Cavagna that fit my friend's description to be found anywhere. If Cavagna was not his real surname, why hadn't Pierre told me—not even when we parted?

Later in life, after serving in the Belgian Army and settling in America, I wrote to agencies in charge of international records. It's as though Pierre never existed.

In my heart, Pierre will always remain *il Professore*. If he is alive and well, I trust that he will remember me affectionately as the English spy.

7167985R10111

Made in the USA
San Bernardino, CA
23 December 2013